CHINESE CROSSWORDS

By Tong Yan and Ying Fu

LONG RIVER PRESS

San Francisco

Published in the United States of America by

Long River Press
360 Swift Avenue
Suite 48
South San Francisco, CA 94080
USA
www.longriverpress.com

First published in 2005 by Cypress Book Co. UK Ltd.
13 Park Royal Metro Centre
Britannia Way
London NW10 7PA

ISBN 10:   1-59265-073-2
ISBN 13:   978-1-59265-073-6

Printed in China

Authors' Foreword

Crossword puzzles need no introduction to Western audiences: they are a well-known, traditional word game played across the English-speaking world. They can be simple or incredibly challenging, depending on the age of the player. Popular board games such as Scrabble®, in which players use the crossword format to create new games each time, continue to be discovered by each new generation. The New York Times Crossword® is world famous and deservedly so: it is devoured by legions of fans eagerly awaiting their paper, and for many it is an established weekend routine.

For more advanced puzzle solvers, crosswords present a special challenge: they can be powerful tools to develop and enhance one's vocabulary. For those learning Chinese language, we saw a unique opportunity, one that has not been addressed before: using crosswords to help teach Chinese and to challenge the reader by helping to boost their vocabulary, knowledge of grammar, and sharpen their sentence construction. Above all else, solving the puzzles should be fun, and we feel they will appeal to the type of reader who has a predisposition for solving crossword puzzles.

It must be pointed out that the idea of *Chinese Crosswords* did not come to us until we were challenged by our students during the Chinese training course. Some of our students were keen on doing English crosswords in the breaks between lessons. One day, a student asked whether we could recommend some easy Chinese crosswords to practice the Chinese he had just learned. At the time we knew of no such work. The idea took off from there and now we hope this book can help both students and anyone interested in Chinese improve their language skills.

We are particularly grateful to Thelma Howell and Edward Dallas for their ideas, advice, and, in particular, their great patience and excellent work on the editing of this book. We are also grateful to all of our students and friends who have tried our practice Chinese crosswords and contributed their invaluable comments and suggestions to the project.

Undoubtedly, it would have been impossible to make our dream of having *Chinese Crosswords* as a book come true without the very kind support of Zhansheng Xia and Xian Xu of Cypress Book Co. UK Ltd in London. We thank them for their encouragement, professional advice, and wholehearted support of teaching Chinese as a foreign language.

It is planned that *Chinese Crosswords* will have three volumes (covering elementary, intermediate, and advanced puzzles). As this is the first volume, there will inevitably be some areas that could benefit from further improvement. We as authors take full responsibility for any such shortfalls. We will be delighted to hear any comments and suggestions for the future improvement of the books.

Tong Yan
Ying Fu

Introduction

It is well known that Chinese is one of the hardest languages in the world to learn. The veritable avalanche of new characters can be daunting and intimidating. Many teachers in this field have been exploring various methods to help students overcome this difficulty. *Chinese Crosswords* aims to offer an alternative way of learning Chinese while offering the reader a series of challenging puzzles. This book has been crafted with the following goals in mind:

• To help further understanding of some of the most often-used words and sentences in specific communicative and social contexts.
• To assist readers in learning more about Chinese culture in association with the language.
• To encourage word association.
• To enlarge vocabulary.
• To practise a very useful skill: guessing in context.
• To be a reference book for teachers in designing vocabulary exercises.

This book is designed following the traditional crossword puzzle format known and beloved by many. It consists of blank boxes in a grid, and clues written in English for Across and Down boxes. The readers are required to fill in the blank boxes so that all the answers line up: they can be words, phrases, or sentences. Unlike English crossword puzzles, you use a Chinese character for each box.

There are 140 crossword puzzles in this book covering about 1,000 items of the most commonly-used words (e.g. 词典), phrases (e.g. 一路平安), and sentences (e.g. 您贵姓). These items are selected based on China's Examination Syllabus of the Chinese Language Standards for Overseas Students 汉语水平考试 (also known as HSK: hàn yǔ shuǐ píng kǎo shì); the Dictionary of Frequency of Use of Chinese Words 汉语频率大辞典, as well as our combined years of empirical experience of teaching Chinese as a foreign language.

An answer key to all of the puzzles is provides at the end of the book, but do not rush straight to the solutions; some mind-searching will help you to retain the solution once found.

This book also shares some close links with many popular textbooks for foundation courses in Chinese as a foreign language used in both China and other countries, such as *Colloquial Chinese, New Practical Chinese Reader, Integrated Chinese, and Practical Audio-Visual Chinese. Chinese Crosswords* can be used as a workbook or even as a supplementary text in association with these textbooks in order to reinforce learning.

This book is designed for almost anyone who knows some basic Chinese. Here are a few tips for readers on how to use the book most effectively:

• Complete the longest word or phrase as soon as possible, as more clues and links will result.
• Read the clues and find the words or phrases that you are certain about before searching for other words.

• Be brave and imaginative; guess possible words using the shared characters you have already filled in.
• Try to make use of any associations to complete the gaps that you have left.
• Some words can be used more than once in different occasions.

References

Beijing Language and Culture University, (1997), China's Examination Syllabus of the Chinese Language Standards for Overseas Students 汉语水平考试 (HSK), Beijing: Modern Publishing House

Beijing Languages Institute, (1986), the Dictionary of Frequency of Use of Chinese Words 汉语频率大辞典, Beijing: Beijing Languages Institute Press

1

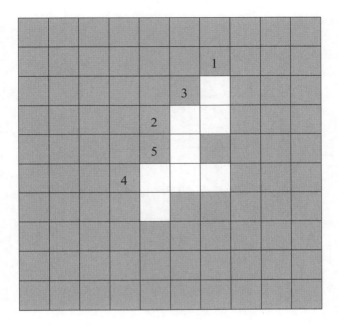

Across
2 The plural form of the first person pronoun
4 A greeting to somebody whom you have not seen for some time

Down
1 The plural form of the second person pronoun
3 An answer to "How are you?"
5 A short question to ask the same thing back to the interlocutor

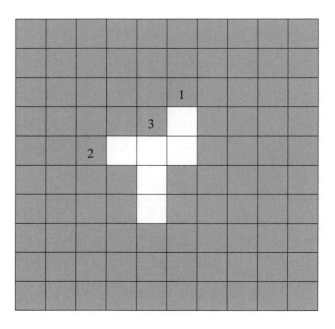

Across

  2   An apology

Down

  1   Together

  3   An answer to "Thank you"

3

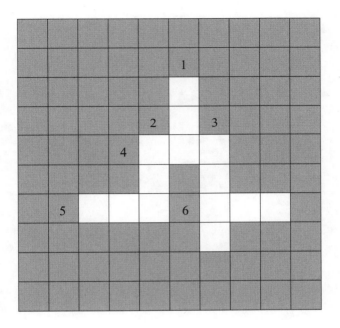

Across

4 The date in a month considered an unlucky date in the West

5 A question used to find out the age of the child you are speaking to

6 Friends who know each other very well

Down

1 The third day of the week

2 The age at which teenagers legally become adults

3 A teacher who teaches Japanese

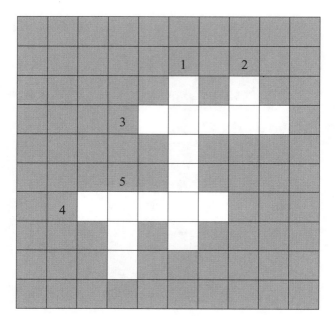

Across

3 A statement to tell other people that he is your younger brother

4 The negative answer to the question "Does she have any sons?"

Down

1 A question to find out if the girl is the daughter of the person you are speaking to

2 The third younger brother

5 The expression people often use to respond to someone's apology

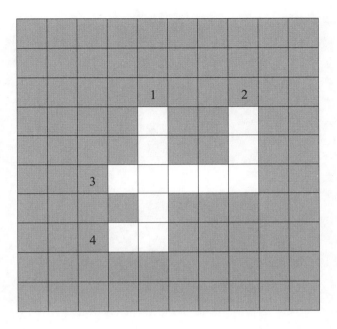

Across

3   A question to find out whether the person you are speaking to would like to drink coffee

4   The name of Chinese black tea

Down

1   A statement saying that you also drink green tea

2   A question to find out whether the person you are speaking to is busy

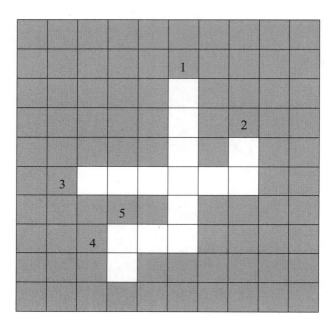

Across

3 A statement you make to tell other people that you mother is a teacher

4 Students at universities

Down

1 A sentence you can use to tell other people that her elder brother is a doctor

2 A person who advises people about laws and represents them in court

5 The eldest brother

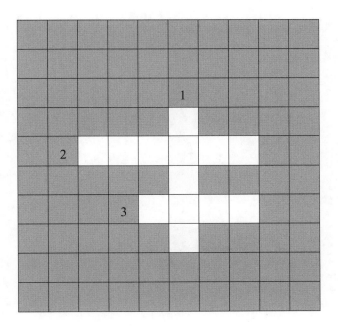

Across

2 A statement to introduce your elder brother to others as a medical doctor

3 A friend from China

Down

1 A question to ask somebody's nationality

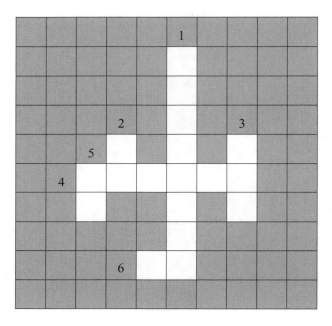

Across

4 A question you use to find out what job the younger sister of the person you are speaking to has

6 To have a meal

Down

1 The statement to tell people that your mother likes cooking Chinese food

2 Sisters of the same parents

3 A question you use to ask for someone's opinion on your suggestion

5 A short follow-up question you can always use if you want to ask the same question as the person ask you

9

Across

2 A common saying used when you meet somebody for the first time

4 A most commonly used greeting

6 A question to ask the person you are speaking to his friend's surname

Down

1 An answer to "How are you?"

3 A question to ask politely somebody's surname

5 A pronoun for the second person plural

7 A greeting used in the morning

10

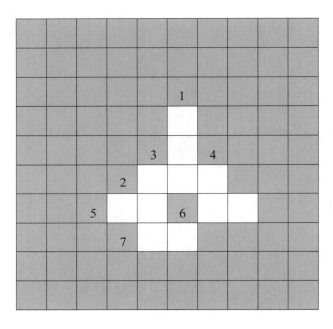

Across

2 A book written in English
5 The name of the country whose capital is Washington
6 A building made for people to live in
7 A place where you can dine

Down

1 To study Chinese
3 Food prepared in a traditional English way
4 A special room in someone's home for reading and writing

11

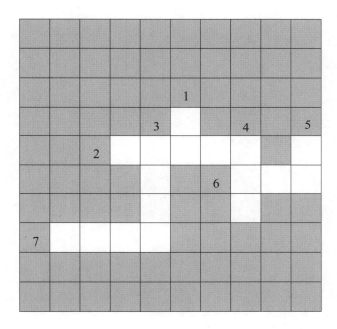

Across
2 The question you use to find out how old the person you are speaking to will be this year
6 People from the same family
7 The date of Childrenís Day in China

Down
1 The year after next
3 A question you use to find out the date today
4 A greeting to everyone present
5 The word for adult

12

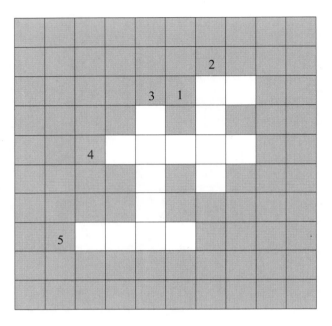

Across
1. The word for this year
4. A question used to ask if the other people are busy or not
5. A question used to ask if the weather is good

Down
2. A statement to say that the weather today is not cold
3. A very positive answer to the question 'how are you both?'

13

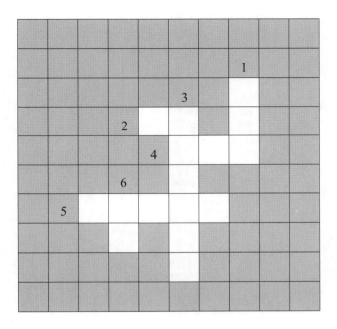

Across

2 The time after dinner today

4 The month that has just past

5 The question you use to find out the time at the moment

Down

1 The last month of the year

3 7:45 p.m.

6 To be at home

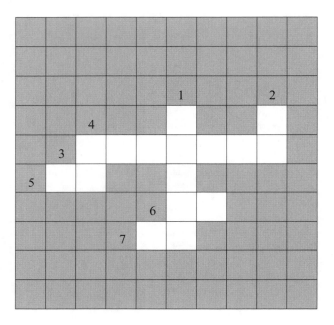

Across

3 An alternative question used to confirm if a man is from Beijing

5 Plural form of the first person pronoun

6 A polite way of addressing a young person whose surname is Zhang

7 Elder daughter of the same parents as oneself

Down

1 A sentence used to introduce Miss Wang to other people

2 The word for husband or wife usually used in mainland China

4 Plural form of the third person pronoun

15

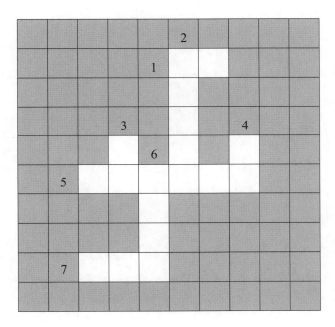

Across
1 The last meal of the day
5 The sentence you use to tell the person you are speaking to that both of you are going to meet up at half past five
7 The last day of the week in Chinese tradition

Down
2 The full word for midnight
3 The plural form of the female third person pronoun
4 The general word people used to say farewell
6 The date of International Labour Day in some countries including China

16

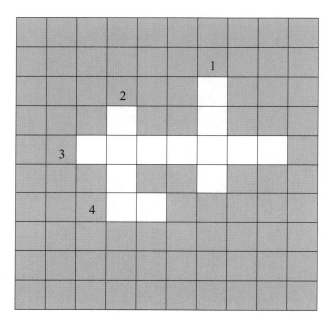

Across

3 A question to ask somebody if he/she is free tomorrow
4 A meal eaten around noon

Down

1 In questions at what time
2 Between lunch and dinner today

17

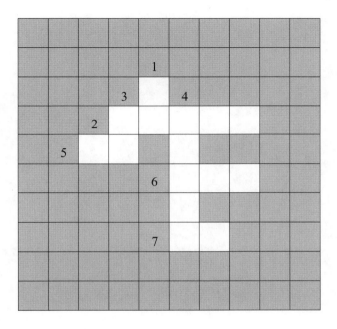

Across

2 The statement you make to tell somebody you are speaking to that you will pay for the meal today

5 The year after next

6 Now and then

7 Assignment given by the teacher in class

Down

1 The day before yesterday

3 The current year

4 The negative answer to the question 'What job have you got?'

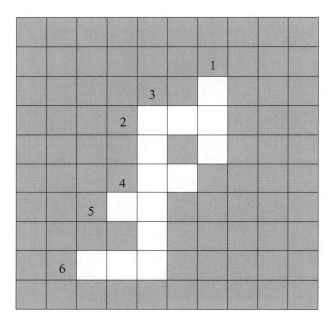

Across

2 A formal way of asking the other person's surname in a conversation

4 The word for both the written and oral Chinese language

5 A country away from your home country

6 A simple question used to find out if the other person is busy

Down

1 A sentence often used to introduce your own family name

3 A simple question used to confirm the nationality of the other person in a conversation

19

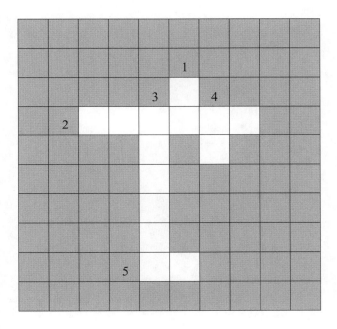

Across
- 2 A statement to present your name card
- 5 The afternoon

Down
- 1 To agree to do something
- 3 A common expression when you start to introduce people
- 4 Words by which a person is known

20

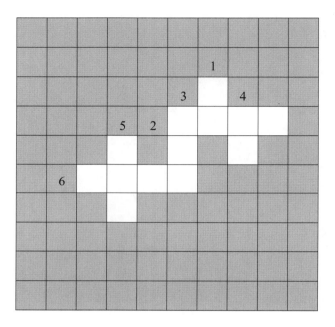

Across
2   Chinese films
6   A question often used before you offer tea to your guest

Down
1   The word for the language most popularly used world-wide
3   The most popular drink in China
4   Television
5   An expression often used to make an apology

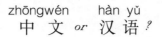

zhōngwén hàn yǔ
中 文 *or* 汉 语 ?

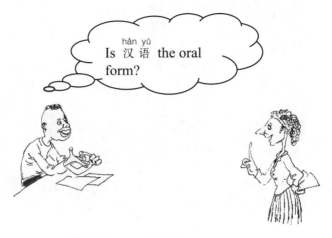

Is 汉 语 (hàn yǔ) the oral form?

A: Do the words 中 文 (zhōngwén) and 汉 语 (hàn yǔ) both mean the Chinese language and are they the same?

B: Yes, the difference is that 中 文 (zhōngwén) is more focused on the written form of the language and 汉 语 (hàn yǔ) on the oral form.

A: Are there any other names for the language

B: Sure, 国 语 (guó yǔ) is the name mainly used in Taiwan and 华 语 (huá yǔ) is more often used in the countries outside of China such as Singapore, Malaysia etc.

21

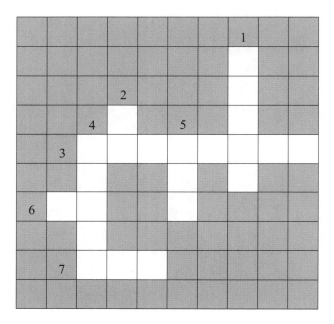

Across
3 The statement telling someone that you often watch TV at the weekend
6 Friends who often play ball games together
7 A title you use to address an unmarried woman whose surname is Li

Down
1 A sentence saying that she likes reading
2 The informal but respectful way to address a senior person whose surname is Zhou
4 The sentence you use to tell other people your friend's surname is Li
5 The short form of a sentence to say that you often go home

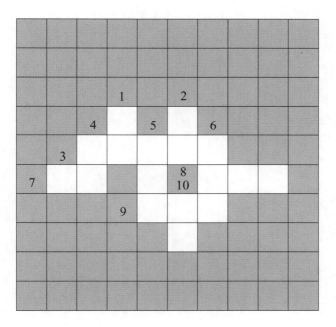

Across

3 A question used to find out the day of the week today
7 The first day of the year
8 A language class in which conversations are practised
9 People from Japan

Down

1 The day before yesterday
2 A date (in general)
4 This year
5 The last day of the week for Chinese people
6 A short question used to ask the number of people in a family
10 An exercise book

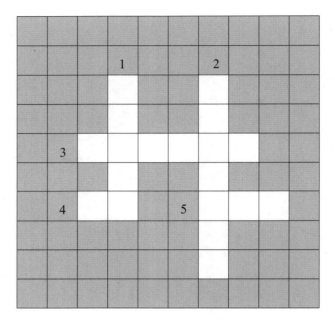

Across

3 A sentence you usually use before you start to make an introduction

4 A short expression in the form of a question often used to show his/her modesty when she/he receives a compliment

5 A short question you can use to inquire about possibility or permission

Down

1 The question you use to find out whether Little Wang has come

2 The sentence you use to express your preference to have a glass of cola after someone has offered you drinks

24

Across
1. A polite way of addressing a senior man whose surname is Wang
3. An expression to show your general satisfation
4. An expression you always use to make an apology
5. A short comment to express your satisfaction with some food
6. To pay a visit to a friend
8. A book written in English
9. The name of the country whose capital is Berlin
10. List of dishes available at a restaurant

Down
2. A statement to show that Mrs Wang dislikes English food
7. To read

25

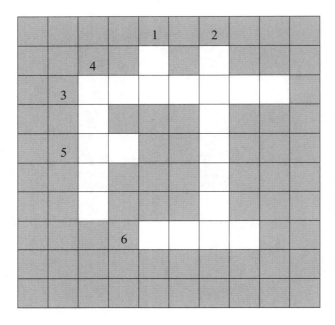

Across
3 A question used to offer water or wine to your guest
5 To have a meal
6 A book store specialising in Chinese books

Down
1 Water that has not been heated
2 A question you use to confirm whether a book belongs to the person whom you are speaking to
4 A question used to ask for the other person's choice of food for a meal

26

Across

1 One of the polite ways to inquire about someone's reaction to your suggestion
5 The question you use to inquire whether the person you are speaking to wants to play the ball game
7 A short sentence you use to request someone to have a look at something
8 A word for "what"

Down

2 An expression people often use when friends meet up again after a long time
3 The question you can use to find out whether he is going to go and see the film or not
4 The ball game people have to play with their feet
6 A question you can use to find out the feelings of the person to whom you are speaking to

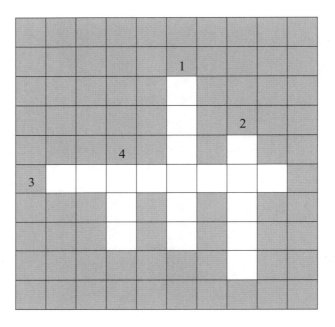

Across

3 A question to find out how many departments there are in your friends' university

Down

1 A question to ask somebody if he has an elder sister
2 Six people from outside of China
4 Somebody who studies in a university

28

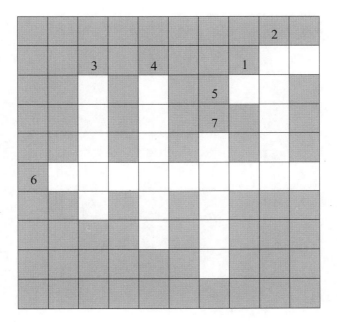

Across
1. The current year
5. The day after today
6. A question to find out when somebody's birthday is

Down
2. A question to find out what day of the week it is today
3. A question asking whose book this is
4. A common wish on somebody on their birthday
7. A question to find out how many students there are

29

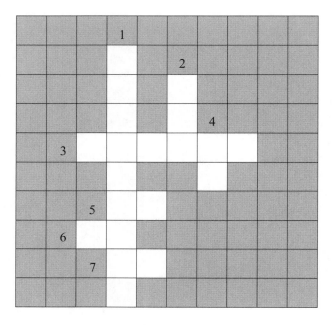

Across

3 A question asking where the person you are speaking to works

5 Stores that sell books

6 A place where meals can be bought and eaten

7 An institution where formal elementary education is given and received

Down

1 A statement saying that she likes studying in the library

2 To have a chat

4 A person who does a job, e.g. in a car factory, etc.

30

Across

1 The first day of a week
3 The day which has just passed
5 A statement saying that you are buying wine in a shopping centre
7 A greeting to everybody

Down

2 A question to find out whether the person you are speaking to will be at home on Sunday.
4 A common drink at a party
6 What you do when you go to a supermarket

31

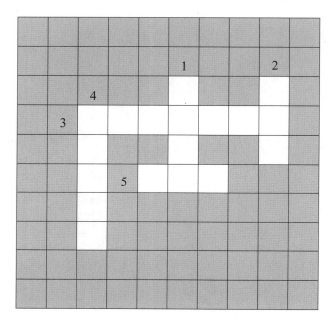

Across

3 A question asking the price of a *Jin* of a apple

5 A polite way of asking somebody's name

Down

1 A complaint saying that the fruit is too expensive

2 Somebody who is rich

4 $8.50 in total

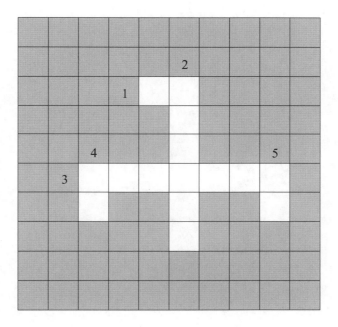

Across

1 A common greeting in the morning

3 A question asking what time of dinner is today

Down

2 A notice saying that the class is going to start at 8a.m.

4 The current year

5 Places where meals can be bought and eaten

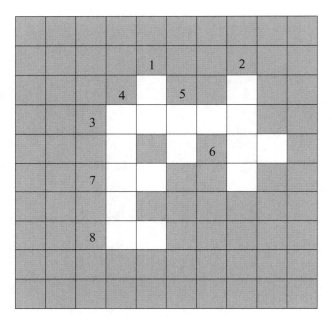

Across

3 A statement to say that I have the ability to speak French
6 Any person over eighty years old
7 To gain knowledge or skill by study
8 Rules for forming words and combining them into sentences

Down

1 A short negative answer to the question "Can you speak Chinese?"
2 A teacher who teaches German
4 A sentence you use to express your desire to learn Chinese
5 To make use of words orally

34

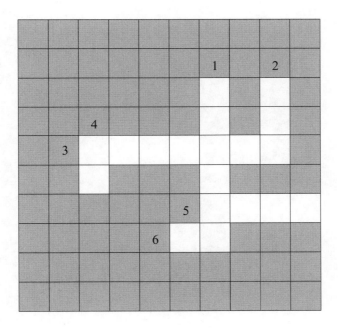

Across
- 3 A polite question asking whether Teacher Wang is in
- 5 A large vehicle that carries the public
- 6 The place where teaching and learning activities take place

Down
- 1 The office of a lawyer whose surname is Li
- 2 A short question to find out what the visitor has come for
- 4 A short expression people use to invite their guest to come in

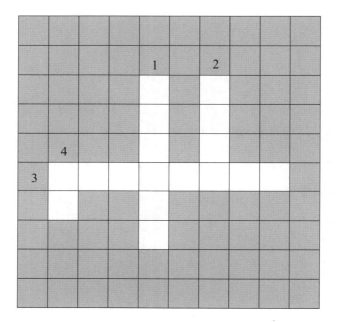

Across

3 A statement telling the teacher that you are not able to come to the class tomorrow

Down

1 A comment saying that it is not easy to learn Chinese
2 A statement saying that he ought to come
4 Next year

36

Across

4 A sentence to say that little Wang is thirty five years old this year

8 An institution that teaches and examines students in many branches of advanced learning

10 The date of Chinese National Day

11 The second day of the weekend

Down

1 A question usually used to ask the age of a child

2 A respectful, but informal way of addressing a senior person whose surname is Wang

3 The coming year

5 The first school for children from around 5 to 11 years of age

6 Today

7 The number of days in a year

9 Day of a person's birth

37

Across

4 A statement saying that you have a meeting this afternoon
9 A place where people drink tea and have refreshments

Down

1 The second day of the weekend
2 12 o'clock in the daytime
3 A party at which people dance to music
5 This evening
6 The coming week
7 An invitation to somebody to come for tea
8 To drive a car

38

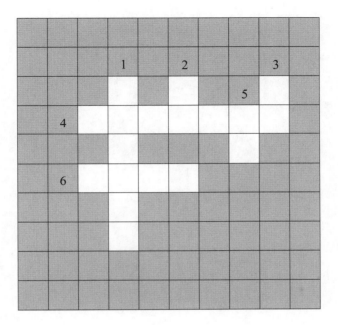

Across

4   A statement saying that he is going to see a doctor in the hospital
6   Two bottles of Cola

Down

1   A way to order a bottle of beer in a restaurant
2   The name of medicine practiced in a traditional Chinese way
3   To be ill
5   Reading a book

39

Across
2 On the day just past
3 Any language that is not used in your own country
6 A question often used to find out the number of people in the family of the person you are speaking to

Down
1 A question used to find out the day of the week today
4 People from a country other than one's own
5 A Chinese family whose head of household is called Wang
7 A question to enquire if there is any Chinese tea
8 A language lesson designed to practise speaking skills

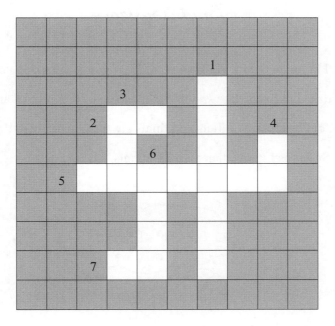

Across

2 Informal word for adults
5 A question asking whether the person you are speaking to
   is available tomorrow
7 A short statement to request two seats in a restaurant

Down

1 A question asking when the person you are speaking to is free
3 A very hot day
4 A short question to confirm whether your suggestion or
   request is accepted
6 A question often used at the beginning of a telephone
   conversation to find out who is calling

Pinyin System

A: I know in the Pinyin system, most of words are made up of initials and finals, like *kan* that is made up of the initial *k* and final *an*, but how many initials and finals are there actually in the system?

B: So far as I know, there are 21 initials and 39 finals.

41

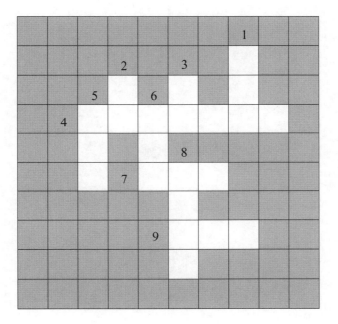

Across

4 A question used to find out if you can speak Shanghai dialect

7 A book about grammar

9 A friend that you have known for a long time

Down

1 The standard official language in China

2 The short negative answer to the question "Can you swim?"

3 Early part of the day before breakfast

5 An expression that you use to offer a seat to a guest

6 To use Chinese language orally

8 A teacher who teachers french

42

Across
3 A statement saying that Teacher Wang asked her to listen to the music
5 A request to somebody not to play ball games
7 Before a meal

Down
1 A statement saying that you are asking Little Wang to call
2 The way in which a particular language is pronounced
4 To listen to a tape recording
6 To tell somebody that he/she must have a meal

43

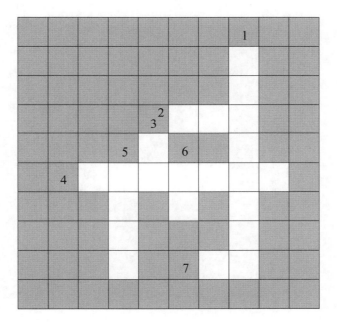

Across
2 A question to find out who that person is
4 A question asking your friend what time he gets up everyday
7 The ball game you play with your feet

Down
1 A question to find out with whom your friend is going to play a ball game
3 The day before yesterday
5 Every week
6 A question you are always asked as soon as you enter a Chinese restaurant with friends

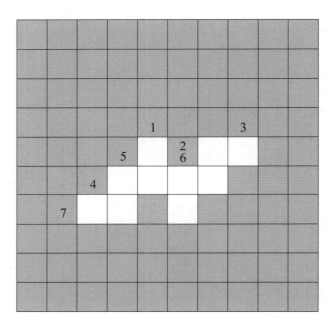

Across

2 First meal of the day
4 Late part of today
7 The year just past

Down

1 A rainy day
3 Early morning
5 The current year
6 A formal way of saying good night

45

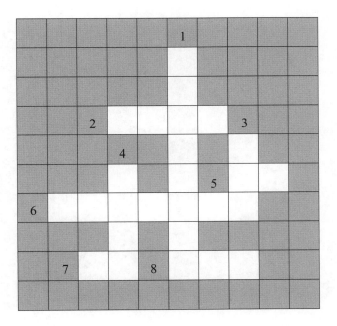

Across

2　To use both Chinese and English
5　A reply you often give when you hear someone saying 'Thanks' to you
6　A very positive comment you make on her handwriting
7　To study again what has been taught
8　A colloquial form of the expression for 'so many people'

Down

1　A compliment you pay to somebody who speaks very good English
3　A short question to ask for someone's opinion about your suggestion
4　An exercise to practise Chinese characters

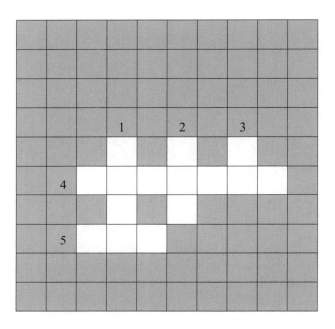

Across

4 A statement saying that you have rented a house

5 A railway station

Down

1 Car with a driver which may be hired

2 To have a look

3 The room in which meals are cooked

47

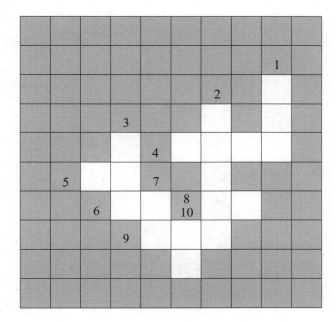

Across

4 A question that a shop assistant usually asks when a customer comes to him/her
5 A general greeting
6 To read
8 A glass or plastic container usually for drinks
9 Wine produced in France

Down

1 A question word to ask for what reason or purpose
2 A sentence that you use in a shop to buy a bottle of wine
3 A short, but positive comment that you might give when you are asked to give your view on the new shoes that your friend just bought
7 Beautiful handwriting
10 A nation or state

48

Across

2 To invite people for dinner

4 The statement saying that he will not come until half past eight

6 The short negative answer to the question 'Have you got married?'

8 People of the same family

9 To have fun

Down

1 The statement saying that you came home as early as 4 o'clock

3 One of the polite ways to ask a guest/visitor to come in

5 The statement saying that he is fairly busy

7 A good-hearted person

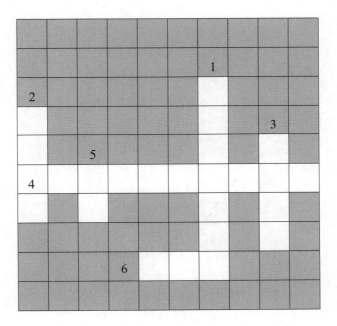

Across

4 A statement saying that Lao Wang has invited you all to have tea at his house

6 The official language spoken in China

Down

1 A negative answer to the question: "Did you phone him?"

2 The teacher who teaches mathematics

3 A question asking what you are going to drink

5 A polite start to a sentence when you want to ask somebody for something

50

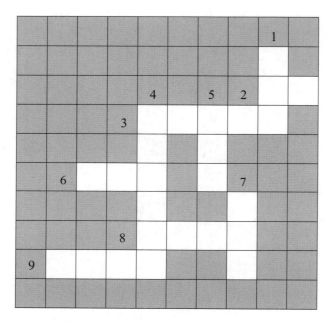

Across

2 An institution for educating children
3 A sentence you use to introduce Mr Li to others
6 A book that people need if they want to learn the German language
8 A question you may use to find out who in a group of people is Zhang Hua
9 A statement to show that you are the owner of the pen

Down

1 Children who go to primary schools
4 A question you use to find out the owner of the book you have found
5 A person with the surname Li who teaches at a school
7 A senior Chinese person who has lived overseas for years

51

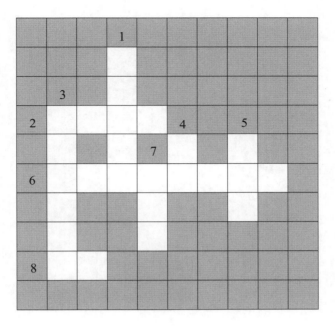

Across

2 The statement saying that you do not drink alcohol
6 A question asking why the person you are speaking to did not go to see the film
8 To produce musical sound with the voice

Down

1 A question asking what the person you are speaking to wants to drink
3 An offer to sing along with the person you are speaking to
4 To go back
5 To make a telephone call
7 A short but positive reply to someone's request for help

52

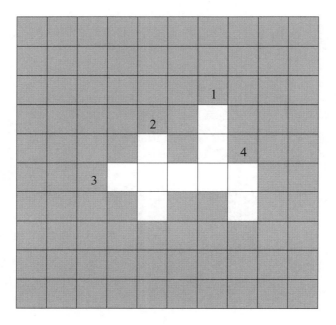

Across
3 A question you use to find out what kind of fish it is before you start eating

Down
1 A question word to find out the reason
2 A question to find out who she is
4 A type of soup made with fish

Across

2 The cold season of the year
4 To hear about
5 The main body of writing in a book such as a textbook
7 A question asking why Little Wang did not come
10 To go back

Down

1 A statement saying that yesterday's lesson was very interesting
3 A question asking somebody to repeat what was previously said
6 The male ruler of a kingdom
8 The formal title that is usually used by unmarried women
9 A short question often used to find out what is happening

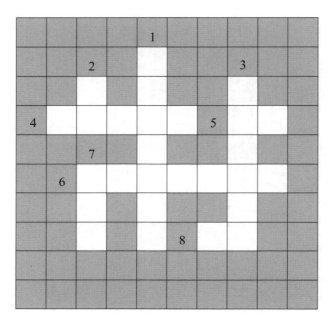

Across

4 A statement saying that he often goes to China
5 Every year
6 A statement saying the teacher is teaching us to write characters
8 A record of something in writing

Down

1 A sentence saying that she teaches Chinese at secondary school
2 Every now and then
3 A statement saying that she writes a diary everyday
7 An old schoolmate

55

Across

2 A form of expression in speech or writing that requests someone to answer

5 To say, write or do something in response to someone's question

7 A statement saying that she has the ability to write letters in Chinese

10 To learn about something through oral communication with other people

Down

1 The language that is mainly spoken in Italy

3 The word for the activity requiring to ask questions and give answers

4 An expression to reply to 'Thank you'

6 To write a letter in reply to the letter or massage you have received

8 The statement saying that she does not speak Japanese

9 The practice of writing Chinese characters

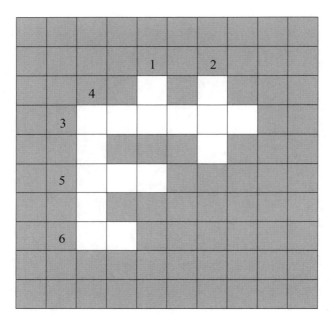

Across

3 A comment you make about a pen before you begin to bargain

5 A form of address to Professor Wang

6 Day of a person's birth

Down

1 A writing instrument that Chinese painters and calligraphers always use

2 The polite form of a question used to ask for the surname of the person you are speaking to

4 A sentence you use to introduce Mr Wang to other people

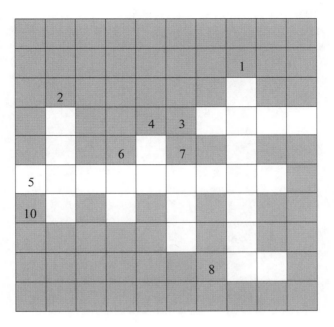

Across

3 The expression you use to tell the host that you must make an earlier departure from the meeting

5 To watch TV immediately after the meal

8 The assignments that teachers give to students to do after class

Down

1 A statement saying that she has no choice but to work with a computer

2 The question asking whether the person you are speaking to has read it

4 In conclusion

6 The time that has gone by

7 A short expression used to indicate that someone is about to come

58

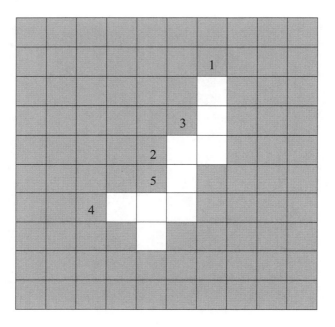

Across

2 The system of transmitting the human voice to a distance by wire or radio

4 An apparatus for receiving sound broadcasting

Down

1 One of the major dialects mainly spoken in Guangdong and Hong Kong

3 An apparatus with a screen and loudspeaker for receiving television broadcasts

5 The art of arranging the sounds of voicesand instruments or both in a pleasing sequence or combination

Across

4 A short question asking whether there is tea or not
5 The citizens of China
6 The national language in France
7 A question to find out what job his girlfriend is doing

Down

1 A question to find out how good someone's Chinese is
2 A statement saying that she has two daughters
3 (Chinese) black tea
8 To make a cake

60

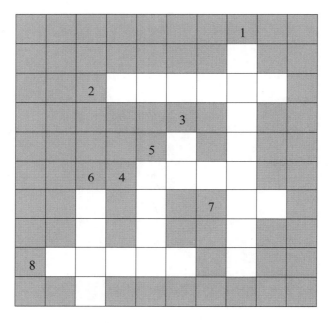

Across
2 A statement saying that Little Li is not in the classroom (shares one of the same characters with 1 Down, but with different tone and meaning)
4 A question used to find out what that thing over there is
7 To write a letter
8 The question often used by teachers asking whether the student has prepared the lesson

Down
1 A statement saying that she teaches me how to write characters (shares one of the same characters with 2 Across, but with different tone and meaning)
3 A word used at the beginning of a clause signalling a shift in the meaning or attitude from the previous clause
5 A short phrase showing that you approve
6 Reports on the weather situation in the near future

Go around China with Mandarin!

A: How many different languages are used in China?

B: Well, apart from Mandarin Chinese (普通话 ^{pǔ tōng huà}) that is used nationally, there are other languages such Tibetan, Mongolian and and so on, as well as many dialects.

A: How many dialects are there in China?

B: I'm not sure, there must be hundreds of them, but I know the seven major dialects are Mandarin 北方, wú 吴, xīang 湘, gàn 赣, Hakka 客家, mǐn 闽 and Cantonese 粤 (or yúe).

61

Across

3 The statement used to tell other people that Little Wang is sixteen years of age this year

7 The elder daughter of the sme parents as oneself

8 The part of the day between 6 p.m. and bedtime.

10 The name of the country whose capital city is Tokyo

12 To prepare food by heating, e.g. frying, boiling

Down

1 The first day of the weekend

2 The year that has just passed

4 A title often used with the name of an unmarried woman

5 The early part of today

6 The date of the Chinese National Day

9 The last meal of the day

11 Books in which you do written homework

62

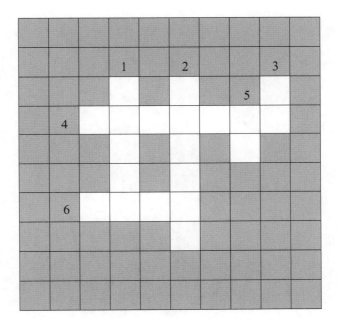

Across

4 A question asking the person you are speaking to whether he can write Chinese characters

6 Textbooks used to learn English

Down

1 A statement saying that he can speak German

2 A statement saying that you know how to cook Japanese food

3 Word or words by which a person is known and spoken to

5 The Chinese Mandarin language

63

Across

3 A short expression used as a rhetorical question to confirm what has been mentioned previously
4 The late part of the day
6 The second meal of the day
7 To entertain guests for dinner at home or in a restaurant
9 A statement saying that she has given me a photo

Down

1 The sentence people often use when they offer their name cards to other people at a meeting
2 The early part of the day around breakfast time
5 A question to find out whether dinner is ready
8 A polite way to request someone to wait a minute
10 An apparatus for taking photographs or moving pictures

64

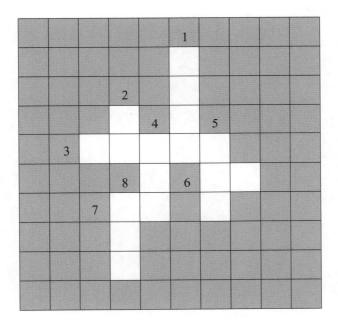

Across

3 A question you use to ask for the price of the apple in a market

6 Printed publications issued daily or weekly containing news

7 Exactly the one or ones referred to or mentioned

Down

1 A question you use to find out what that is

2 A word for fruit

4 A question that Chinese people often use to greet each other informally

5 A person who sells newspapers

8 The smallest denomination of the Chinese currency RMB

65

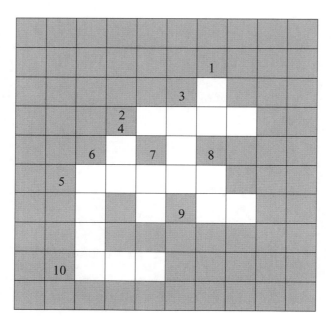

Across

2 To have an English lesson
5 A question asking who can play tennis
9 Fellow players in the same team
10 One of the ways of saying good-bye

Down

1 The oral form of a language
3 The internet
4 To hold a meeting
6 The question asking who Li Ming is
7 To write something with a computer or typewriter
8 A team for any type of ball game

66

Across

1 Shopping
5 A statement saying that they are in the middle of practising speaking Chinese
7 Schools for girls
9 A dictionary with which you find out English words from Chinese words
10 The word that someone or something is called or known by

Down

2 The language spoken in Spain and some South American countries
3 A group of students
4 To learn to write Chinese characters
6 Being at school
8 A girl companion with whom a boy or man spends time and shares amusements

67

Across
2   A question asking what is for lunch
5   A statement saying that there is no need to take the medicine
6   A statement saying that your friend is the manager of a company
8   The word for stuff

Down
1   The time of the day before lunch
3   A question to offer a choice between having Chinese medicine or western medicine
4   A statement saying that this is not mine
7   The study of the production, distribution and use of goods and wealth

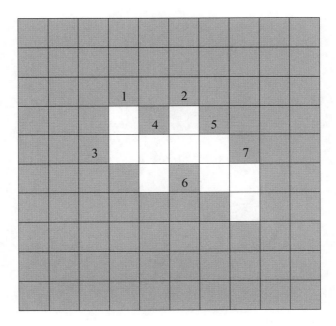

Across

3 Between 6 p.m. and bedtime everyday

6 The second meal of the day

Down

1 The day following today

2 The late part of today

4 Conditions of the atmosphere at a certain place and time

5 The early part of the day before lunch

7 The table at which you have meals at home

69

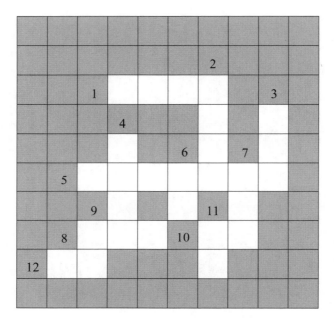

Across

1 Queen Elizabeth II
5 The statement saying that the speaker is going to a friend's house for fun
8 The eldest son of the same parents
10 The organ of the body controlling thought and feeling
12 a long-sleeved outer garmment worn on the upper part of the body

Down

2 The home of Teacher Wang
3 To have a chat
4 A question commonly used as a daily greeting
6 To be friendly
7 To play on the computer
9 A long warm coat worn over other clothes by men and women in cold weather
11 Heavy rain

70

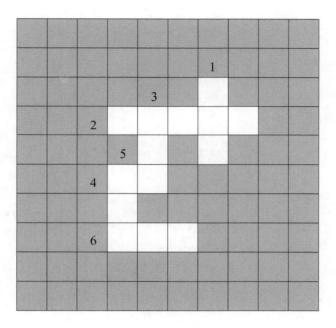

Across

2 A statement you make to say that you cannot drink alcohol

4 A short and informal expression you can use to express your gratitude

6 An excuse you sometimes give if you do not want to buy something or you do not have enough money

Down

1 A polite way to offer your guest tea

3 One of the common replies you hear when you say 'thank you' to someone

5 A question you usually use to find out how much you need to pay for your shopping

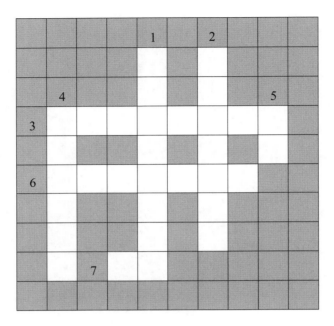

Across

3 A statement saying that he often helps me to practise the spoken language

6 A question asking those who went to the party what kind of alcohol they drank

7 The word for pencil

Down

1 A statement saying that he bought a pen for you

2 A question asking a university student what major he/she is studying

4 A question to find out if the man is the elder brother of the person you are speaking to

5 Rules for forming words and making sentences

72

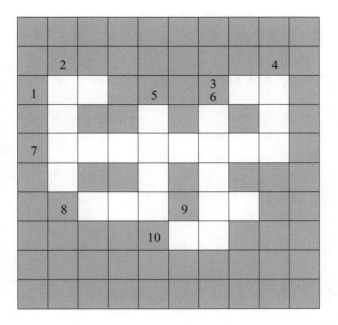

Across

1 A short form of the question reciprocating the original question you answered
3 Southeast
7 The statement saying that he is currently talking with the teacher
8 A polite way to ask someone to come in
9 A public garden
10 A room for someone to sleep in

Down

2 Advice to go to ask him
4 The dialect mainly spoken in Nanjing
5 A request asking someone to follow the speaker
6 The office of the lawyers

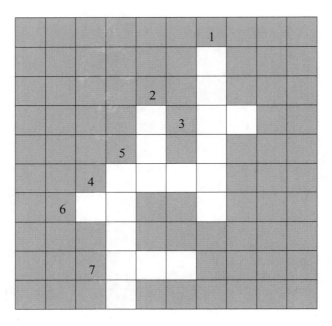

Across

3 A small instrument showing the time worn on the wrist
4 A question you use to find out what a girl's surname is
6 At all times
7 One of the most popular martial in China using slow movements

Down

1 A question you use to show your concern when you have noticed that something is wrong with your friend's hand
2 The polite way to find out the surname of the person you are speaking to
5 A sentence you use to tell other people that she is Mrs Li

Across

1 A very polite greeting to somebody in the morning
3 An apology when you arrive late
7 A compliment saying that young people speak very fluent English
8 An expression for "long time no see"

Down

2 A question asking the age of a person over 70
4 A common question to be asked when somebody wants to find out if you sleep well at night
5 A phrase which refers to people from other countries
6 A comment saying that Japanese is not easy to learn

Across

5   A statement giving permission to somebody to do their coursework on a computer

7   The word for 'but' or 'yet'

8   To be joyful

9   A short follow-up question to confirm the suggestion someone has raised

Down

1   A telephone with a recording device

2   A lesson in which music is taught

3   The word used at the beginning of a clause to signal that the result follows

4   The question asking whether the meal is ready

6   One of the most popular soft drinks in the world

10 Friends with very close relationships

76

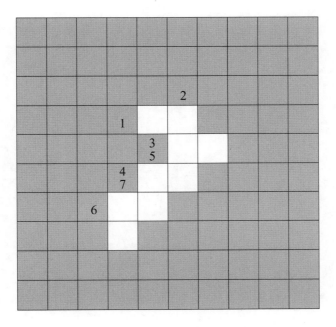

Across
1 For the reason that
3 A question word showing surprise or needing a repeat
4 In what way or manner
6 Not different

Down
2 A question word used to find out for what reason or purpose an action is done
5 In what way
7 To indicate obligation or advice

Across

2 A statement saying that he lives in the north of the UK
5 A question to find out whether Shanghai people speak Putonghua
6 A statement saying that Chinese grammar is very easy

Down

1 A statement saying that she speaks very fluent English
3 A statement saying that he does not go to the oral language classes
4 The Beijing dialect

78

Across

2 A musical performance given by a number of singers or musicians
4 The month just passed
5 To be cute
7 The expression people often use to wish someone a happy birthday
11 To revise what has been taught

Down

1 Being at the meeting
3 The date for Chinese Army Day
6 The short form of the word for a very popular soft drink
8 An expression usually used at the end of a letter to express the hope that someone's studies are going well
9 Words that have not yet been learnt
10 A passenger train that does not stop at every station, only at big cities

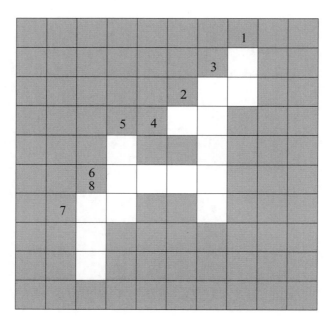

Across

2 The plural form of the third person pronoun
4 On the condition that
6 The warning that says no smoking is allowed
7 Together or in company

Down

1 The plural form of the first person pronoun
3 The statement that says he is the person who sells cigarettes
5 The most popular expression used to make an apology
8 An expression used to describle a small amount

80

Across

2 The teacher's house
3 The art of beautiful handwriting
4 A building where goods are sold
8 A statement saying that he has just come back to the U.S. from China
9 An expression to indicate you are really sorry

Down

1 A comment saying that there are not many Chinese language books in this bookstore
5 A statement to say that you have to go home
6 A claim saying that you have just arrived
7 The name of the country of which Washington DC is the capital

3000 characters will do!

A: How many characters are there in the Chinese language?

B: It's difficult to give you a definite number because different dictionaries have different numbers of characters, e.g. kāngxī *Dictionary* has 47,035 characters, zhōngwén *Big Dictionary* (Taiwan) has 49,905, and hànyǔ *Big Dictionary* has 56,000.

A: Oh, my God, how on earth can I manage to learn all of them? Never.

B: Don't worry; there are many words that are not often used. According to the research, there are only 3,000-4,000 characters that are commonly used. This means you should be able to read Chinese newspapers if you know around 3,000 characters

A: Really? That's good news!

81

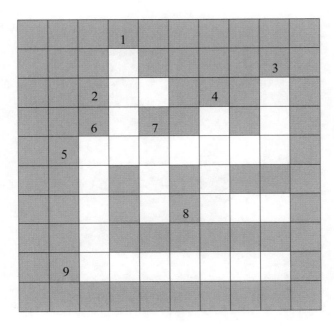

Across

2 Your views on a person or situation
5 A statement saying that you want to buy a shirt
8 Waiters or waitresses (more often used in Taiwan)
9 The sentence used by the shop assistant when he/she gives you $5.67 in change

Down

1 An expression you use to think about something before you give any view or make any decision
3 Sports clothes
4 Two items of clothing
6 A statement used by shop assistant saying that they will go and have a look for you
7 Shopping

82

Across

3 A question you may use to find out whether the person you are speaking to can write Chinese characters

6 A book that gives instruction in a subject

8 To gain knowledge or skill through study

10 One of the often used expressions in a restaurant if you want to order a whole fish

Down

1 A form of exercise in a language class in which the teacher reads aloud and students write down what s/he reads

2 A word or words by which a person, an animal or a thing is known

4 A type of language exercise to practise speaking skills

5 The occasion when a student or a group of students meet to learn Chinese

7 Originally

9 An institution where people can receive formal education

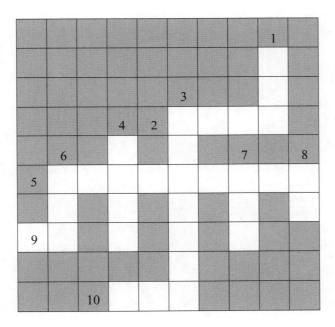

Across

2 The negative answer to the question "Do we need to stand in line?"

5 A statement saying that many people come to study in the U.S. from abroad

9 A short greeting said in the morning

10 A dialect mainly spoken in Guangdong Province

Down

1 A soccer team

3 A statement saying that there is no need to learn Mandarin

4 Bank of China

6 A comment to somebody who came early

7 The Chinese currency

8 A short expression for "many thanks"

84

Across

2 People who receive education or professional training in schools or universities
4 Every week
6 A statement saying that the pair of pants costs $53
7 Thirty minutes
10 The bed designed for two people to sleep on

Down

1 He gets up at 5.30 a.m. every day
3 Any of the three or four periods in the year in which classes are held in schools or universities
5 An outer garment covering both legs and reaching from the waist to the ankles
8 All the years of the past, present and future
9 Two pairs of shoes

85

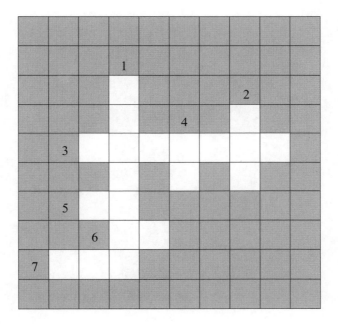

Across
3 A comment that says the work he is doing is very difficult
5 The word for any other countries away from your home country
6 A place where you can pay to have food and drink
7 A question you use to show your concern as to whether the person you are speaking to is tired

Down
1 A question you use to find out whether the person you are speaking to can cook Chinese food
2 The most often used reply to the question 'how are you'
4 A person who works in a factory

86

Across
- 2 A response to "Thank you"
- 6 A comment saying that this library is really big
- 9 Period of 60 minutes
- 10 To go to the cinema

Down
- 1 Condition of sun, wind, temperature, etc at a particular area and time
- 3 Not very big
- 4 Every
- 5 The time for returning books
- 7 A comment to make when you are surprised at the small size
- 8 An exclamation saying that something looks very good
- 11 The method of broadcasting pictures and sound over a distance by means of electrical waves

87

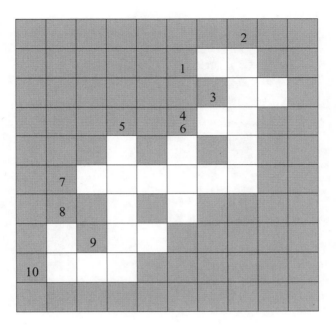

Across

1 The short form of the negative answer to the question 'Is the dictionary on your desk?'
3 A short, polite form of response to someone's praise
4 Female children
7 A statement saying that this is $200
9 Goods
10 People who work in shops and restaurants (more often used in mainland China)

Down

2 A question asking where you make payment
5 A question asking who is the shop assistant
6 A century
8 A general term for all garments

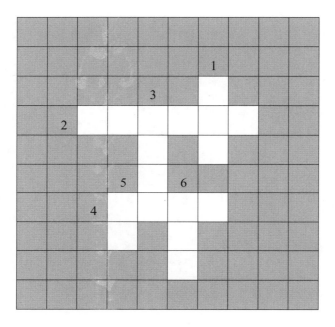

Across

2 The statement you make to tell other people that you can only speak French

4 To gain knowledge and skills of Chinese language

Down

1 The lesson in which grammar is taught

3 Language exercises for conversational skills

5 An institution where formal education can be given and received

6 Students who study in secondary schools

89

Across

2 Her spouse (mainly used in mainland China)
4 The word used at the beginning of a clause giving reasons
6 The question a shop assistant often uses to find out what colour the customer likes
8 To be both tall and big
10 A symbol or word indicating a size, quantity, house, telephone number

Down

1 A beautiful person
3 A question asking why she is not happy
5 Yellow color
7 To be joyful
9 A large size

Across

2 To finish class
4 12:00 noon
6 To say 'because it is too hard' as the reason why you gave up learning Chinese
8 The word for "in that case" which is often used in negotiation
10 Unpleasant to look at
12 In what place
13 A shop that sells books

Down

1 To go to class
3 The second part of the day before supper
5 A question that is used to find out whether Chinese language is difficult
7 A question word used to find out the reasons
9 In that place
11 To read

91

Across

1 To bake bread
4 A statement saying that you are good at playing ball games
6 A statement saying that he has a Chinese name
9 A common way to refer to computers
10 An expression for "not big"

Down

2 A statement saying that roast duck is very famous
3 The word for soccer
5 A statement saying that you will phone him
7 A form of writing valued as works of art
8 A statement saying that the characters is too big

92

Across
2. A statement saying you are going to look for him
4. Every now and then
5. A short sleep around lunch time
7. A statement saying the pair of shoes is too big
10. A small bed

Down
1. A suggestion that the person you are speaking to should go
3. A statement saying he has already gone to bed
6. Soft rubber-soled shoes worn by people while exercising
8. Double bed
9. An expression often used in bargaining over a price

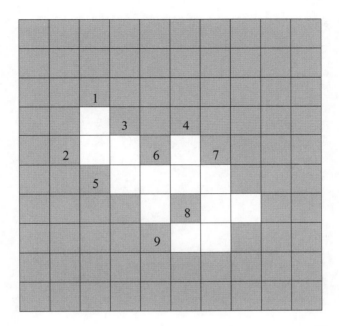

Across

2 To go up the mountain
5 The four points of the compass
8 The way that a person or thing faces
9 Informal talks

Down

1 The late part of the day
3 The name of the province in China, whose capital city is Jinan
4 The name of the autonomous region in the southern part of China, whose capital city is Nanning
6 The name of the city that used to be the capital of China before 1949
7 The dialect that is mainly spoken in the northern part of China

Across

3 A statement saying there are a lot of questions to ask
6 A statement saying that there is a master with the surname Wang
9 A colloquial way of saying to teach
10 A compliment saying that it is a good place to study

Down

1 A comment saying that it is not much
2 A short expression you always use to start a query
4 A statement saying that there are many famous films
5 A suggestion to ask the teacher
7 Professor Wang
8 Primary schools
11 Representation of the earth surface for the whole or a part of the area

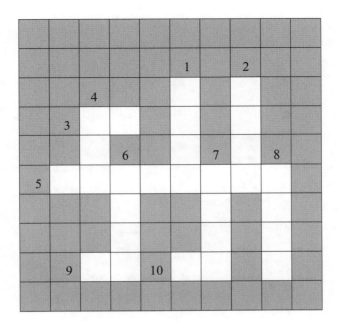

Across

3   The word for next time
5   A statement saying that you do not want to go to class today
9   The word for green tea
10 The first season in the year

Down

1   To tell the person you are speaking to to think about it
2   To be on the plane
4   The day when it rains
6   To say that you want to drink tea
7   Autumn last year
8   The exercises assigned by the teachers for students to do after class

Across

1 A polite nickname that many Chinese people call foreigners

4 The language that is mainly spoken in the country whose capital is Paris

6 The Peoples' Republic of China

10 A question you use to find out where the library is

Down

2 The word for anyone who is not from your home country

3 In total

5 The name of the country whose capital city is Paris

7 The map that describes geographical locations of China

8 A public place where meals can be bought and eaten

9 Flowers

11 A store that sells books

12 An often used Chinese expression in reply to praise in public

97

Across

2 A statement saying that somebody slept at home for three days

5 A statement saying that there is still nothing in the house

7 An expression for "sold out"

9 To borrow books

Down

1 A statement saying that you have not yet finished learning Lesson Three

3 In the park

4 A question to find out how well the person you are speaking to slept

6 The rent for the house

8 To sell books

Across

1 A colloquial word for trading
5 The question used by shop assistants asking what size of shoes the customer wears
9 A short skirt
10 The general term for senior people

Down

2 A person who sells vegetables
3 Children
4 A short question to find out the date
6 The person who is wearing a red skirt
7 A shop specialising in selling hats and shoes
8 The first year at university

Across

4 A sentence that is used to say that Shanghai is in the eastern part of China

8 An institution where specialised subjects are taught and studied

10 Next to someone or something

11 Male children of parents

Down

1 The part in the northwest

2 Big ocean

3 The name of the country whose capital city is Berlin

5 To go to primary school

6 To be/stay at home

7 The southeastern area

9 Everyone

100

Across
4 A statement saying that an exam took place last week
6 A short question asking which month it is
7 A short statement saying that you have completed filling in the form
8 A suggestion meaning "let's go"
9 A statement used when you finish doing something
10 A compliment about the good wine

Down
1 A suggestion to have a go at doing something
2 A statement saying that he left last month
3 The word for the date
5 A question to find out how somebody did in an exam

How Many Radicals?

A: I've been told that in learning characters, radicals are very important, because they give a clue to the meaning of the word. But I'm wondering how many radicals there actually are in the writing system?

B: I can't give you a difinite number because the number of radicals varies from one dictionary to another. But it is generally agreed that there are about 200.

101

Across
5 A statement saying that her car is the same as yours
7 Schools that only accept girl students
8 To communicate orally
9 4 o'clock sharp
10 The beginning of the year

Down
1 To tell someone to buy a good one
2 A question word often used as a greeting
3 A question asking where the school of the person you are speaking to is
4 A request language teachers often use to ask someone to repeat something after her/him
6 The year of the founding of the People's Republic of China

102

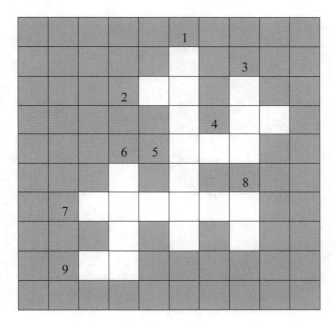

Across
2 The day before yesterday
4 Train or bus ticket
5 A work place where people study and predict weather situations
7 A question that you always use to find out the name of the person you are speaking to
9 To find something or somebody pleasant

Down
1 A question that you usually use to find out what the weather is like today
3 The place where you take the bus
6 A sentence that you use to introduce yourself as Wang Huan
8 A thick book that has a good collection of Chinese characters and their meanings

103

Across
4 A statement saying the office is on the fifth floor
6 Inside the shop
7 A statement meaning there is no way to sort it out
9 A question asking what is good about playing tennis
10 A conjunction that indicates the consequence

Down
1 A short question for "What shall we do?"
2 A statement saying Friday is best for a grammar lesson
3 The room in which people sleep and have a rest
5 A question to find out whether there is a toilet in the park or not
8 To surf the Internet

104

Across

4   A statement saying that the book belongs to Little Wang
6   On the floor
7   To go abroad to study
8   A general term for all garments
9   A type of tea that is scented
11 The statement saying that it is such a beautiful park

Down

1   The statement saying that he is not American
2   A book giving instruction in a subject
3   Another word for Queen
5   A question often used to find out the price of a coat
10 A public or private garden growing flowers

105

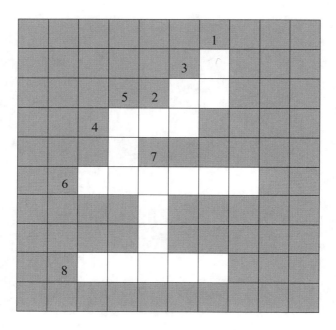

Across

2   Mental activities to gain knowledge and skills
4   A public place where films are shown
6   A question you use to find outwhat he says in the letter
8   A statement saying that English lessons are not difficult

Down

1   Activities or tasks intended for mental or physical training
3   Institutions for higher education or professional training
5   The word for 'e-mail'
7   To have a Chinese lesson

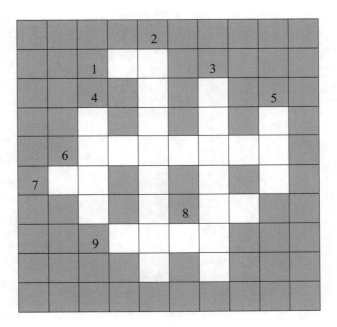

Across

1 The number 50
6 A statement saying that half an hour has already passed
7 The word for being late
8 A short question asking how many or how much something is
9 A comment saying that the living room is very big

Down

2 A statement that you will see somebody at 12:30 in the dining hall
3 A question you use to find out how old your friend's child is
4 A short message to your friend saying that you have arrived home
5 A greeting often used when you see somebody after dinner

107

Across
1 The dialect mainly used by the people of Shanghai
5 A statement saying that the grammar in Chapter 9 is difficult
7 A special report predicting the weather situation
10 To be allowed to
12 An expression often used on someone's birthday

Down
2 The first day at school
3 The language mainly spoken in the country whose capital is Moscow
4 An expression saying that something is too difficult
6 Rules regulating the behaviour of members of a country
8 To study new words before class
9 The word used at the beginning of a clause leading to a result
11 The short form of the brand name of one of the most popular soft drinks in the world

108

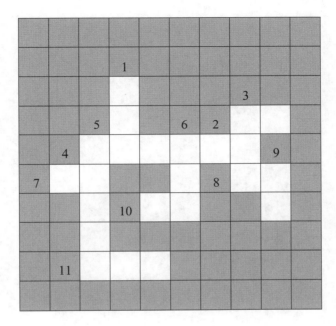

Across

2   A polite way to invite a visitor to enter your room or office

4   A negative comment that says the bottle of spirits is no good

7   A word you use to change or modify your ideas in conversation or writing

8   A cup or glass that people often use for Chinese tea

10 One of the often used short expreeions to say thank you

11 The short form of the sentence you use to say that the thing you want to buy is too big

Down

1   The bottle that contains milk

3   An expression you often use to offer tea to guests

5   A sentence you use to introduce Mrs Wang to other people

6   One of the replies to the expression 'thank you'

9   A cup or glass people use for general purposes

109

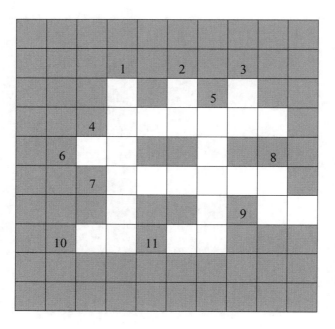

Across

4   A statement saying that something was posted from the USA
6   To take part in
7   A request to take 25 books
9   Building made for people to live in
10   To come out
11   To write letters

Down

1   A statement saying that somebody has just come here from Canada
2   To go abroad
3   To come back
5   A statement saying that 5 letters were posted
8   A room used for reading, writing, etc.

110

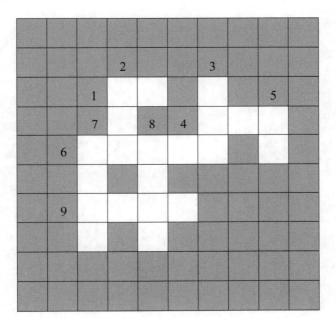

Across

1 An expression for a negative comparison, e.g. "not as good as"
4 To make a calculation
6 To remind somebody to give the money to the driver
9 A statement saying that there is another one (one of the characters is shared with 7 Down but with different pronunciation)

Down

2 A negative answer to the question "Do I need to pay?"
3 An electronic device for storing, analysing and producing information
5 A short expression meaning "forget it" or "leave it"
7 A suggestion saying that the book was returned (one of the characters is shared with 9 Across but with different pronunciation)
8 A request to give him one copy

111

Across

4 A statement saying that the train is faster than the bus
7 An adverb indicating that something has happened before the present time
9 A short phrase referring to somebody who sells tickets
10 A statement saying that something has been done

Down

1 Still a popular method of transportation in China
2 Places outside of your local area
3 The amount obtained when several smaller amounts are added together
5 The office of the company manager
6 A liquid used as a fuel for cars and other vehicles
8 A brief statement saying that he has left
11 A word for a matter

112

Across

1. A phrase for three questions
4. A statement saying "let him go next month"
8. To go upstairs
9. To take part in
10. An office
11. The word for beautiful
12. The making of something expressive or beautiful

Down

2. A duration of three months
3. A suggestion that you go and ask him
5. A suggestion to go downstairs to get on with the business
6. A positive answer to "Shall we ask him to come?"
7. A suggestion to go and visit the art gallery

113

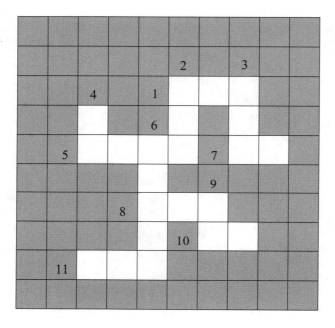

Across

1 A suggestion to try to listen
5 A wish often said before a weekend (one of the characters is shared with 2 Down but with different pronunciation)
7 A positive answer to "Have you understood?"
8 A statement saying that nothing can been seen
10 A word for an interview when you apply for a job
11 A Tennis match

Down

2 A phrase for listening to the music (one of the characters is shared with 5 Across but with different pronunciation)
3 A negative statement after you listened to something and did not understand
4 An expression for last week
6 A suggestion to go quikly to watch the match
9 The word for to meet

114

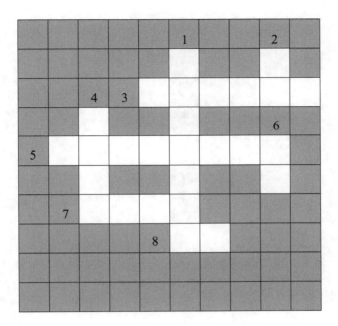

Across

3   Two Chinese – English dictionaries
5   A comment saying that this shirt is longer than the other one
7   Textbooks for physics
8   The formal form of the word "your country" used in a diplomatic occasion

Down

1   A statement saying that this book is more expensive than the other one
2   A word for the words one has not yet learned
4   A present
6   A word for long skirts

115

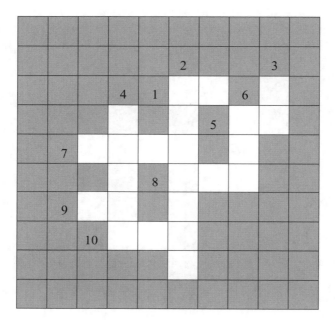

Across
1 To set off
5 A system of transmitting the human voice by wire or radio
7 A new car
8 To fly an airplane
9 To travel
10 A statement used when you see a bus or taxi is coming

Down
2 A statement saying that the taxi has gone down the wrong road
3 A general word indicating the activity of speaking
4 Five bicycles
6 An apparatus for receiving television broadcasts

116

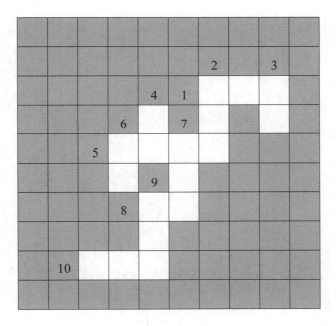

Across
1 To go through the process of getting a passport
5 A classroom designed specialy for teaching music (one of the characters is shared with 4 Down but with different pronunciation)
8 To write characters
10 A short statement saying that you have understood what you heard

Down
2 A room where people work
3 Pictures taken with cameras
4 Feeling pleasure, contentment, satisfaction, etc. (one of the characters is shared with 5 Across but with different pronunciation
6 Message or news
7 To teach Chinese characters
9 A comment saying that what has been written is wrong

117

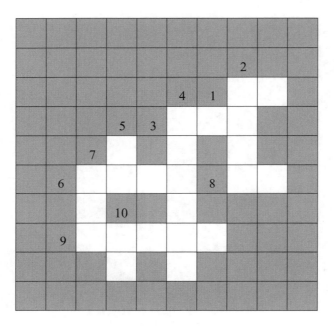

Across
1. A phrase to express immediateness
3. A phrase indicating the continuous action of riding a horse
6. To travel by bus, train or taxi
8. The year of the Tiger
9. To take the lift to go upstairs

Down
2. An expression with the meaning "not so bad, not so good; just so-so"
4. To ride a bicycle to go to work
5. The word for cars
7. An expression mearning to sit for a while
10. A tram

118

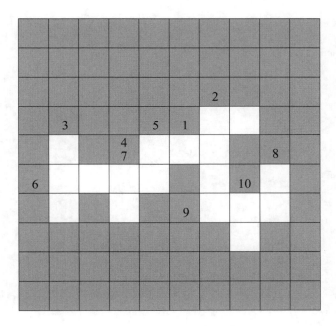

Across
1 A word giving permission
4 To make a joke
6 To go to a concert
9 The name of the Chinese currency

Down
2 A funny person
3 A typical Chinese saying indicating that somebody is not following what he was told
5 To hold a meeting
7 Musical instruments
8 Foreign currency
10 The word for a nation

119

Across

2 The right hand of a person
4 A statement saying that the toilet is on the left
7 To drink water
8 The people who are invited
9 A phrase for ordinary
10 A place where people have meals
11 To raise, increase or improve

Down

1 Part of a building with its own walls, ceiling and door
3 A statement saying that the living room is on the right
5 A statement saying that living standards are high
6 A short question asking "where"

120

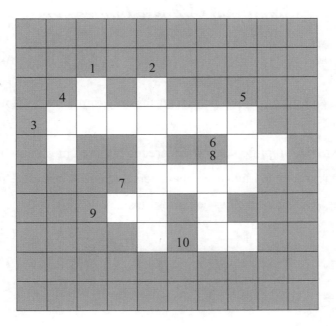

Across

3　A statement saying that it is very busy when school starts
6　Business organizations
7　A statement saying that something has been done wrongly (one of the characters is shared with 8 Down but with different pronunciation)
9　What somebody does in orfer to earn money
10　To get up

Down

1　To go to school
2　A statement saying that there is time to do the assignments set by the teacher
4　To open the door
5　Being busy with business
8　A compliment meaning amazing, terrific, extraordinary, etc. (one of the characters is shared with 7Across but with different pronunciation)

Simplified Chinese Charecter?

A: Is simplified Chinese character the only form of writing now in use?

B: No, the simplified characters are mainly used in Chinese mainland, but the traditional full-form characters are more often used in Hong Kong, Taiwan as well as countries outside of China.

教汉语

教漢語

121

Across

3 A statement saying that university students all read newspapers
6 A statement saying that the office building is not far from the customs house
9 The ground for soccer games
10 Many days later

Down

1 Secondary school
2 Daily newspapers
4 A statement saying that the university is a long way away from the shopping centre
5 To have foresight
7 To do business
8 To close the door
11 At the back

122

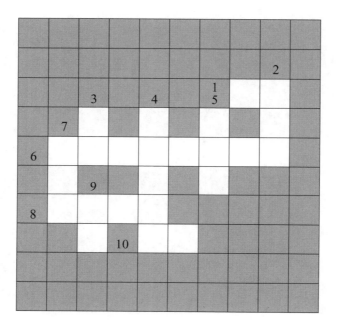

Across

1 The formal title for a man
6 A statement saying that the star actor performed extremely well
8 A description of (a person having) a friendly and easy manner
10 A building in which plays are performed

Down

2 To be angry
3 The owner of the house
4 To perform local operas
5 Advice to hold and take good care of the tickets
7 A boyfriend
9 A good person

123

Across

3 A common wish to somebody at New Year
6 An expression used to persuade somebody not to be worried
8 To be extremely busy
10 On condition that
11 To have the same opinion as somebody else
12 To be an interpreter or translator

Down

1 A traditional phrase meaning "to spend the year"
2 Music (sharing the same character as 3 Across but with different pronunciation
4 May all your wishes come true
5 Advice to run fast
7 To hurry
9 A polite reply when you receive a compliment

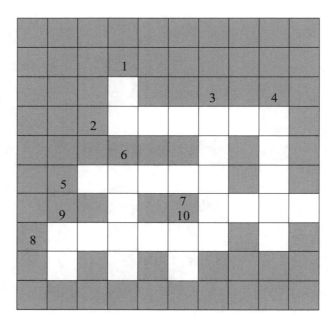

Across

2 A statement saying that the melody is especially fine
5 A statement saying that somebody has gone to watch the Peking opera
7 To take the map
8 A statement saying that one has never given money

Down

1 A musical composition
3 Advice not to forget to take some money
4 A compliment for a beautiful plce
6 A short question asking whether the peoson has seen the thing
9 Once upon a time
10 In the past

125

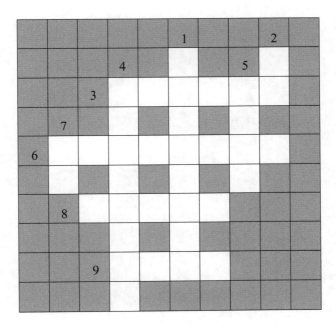

Across

3 A notice advising you to use the elevator when going up or down stairs

6 A statement saying that there is a shop beside the post office

8 To go home for one month

9 A garden in the Chinese style

Down

1 A statement saying that there is a garden behind the big building

2 Stairs

4 A statement saying that the country at the top (of a map) is China

5 Shops that sell electric devices

7 Stickers to show that postage has been paid

126

Across
1 To cross the road
6 A comment saying that it is too formal
8 A statement saying that the weather is very hot
10 To not be accustomed to

Down
2 To celebrate a festival
3 A complaint saying that it was too hot on the way
4 To be ill
5 Cold days
7 The styles (of clothes)
9 A statement saying that the temperature is not high

127

Across
- 3   To buy a house
- 5   A kind of pen used to practice calligraphy
- 6   A statement saying that you are two centimeters taller than I am
- 9   A statement saying that something was bought on the same day
- 11   A shop where flowers are sold

Down
- 1   A price of $0.35
- 2   A common expression when you share somebody's pleasure at success, good fortune, etc. and give them your congratulations
- 4   A statement saying that the house rent is high
- 7   A statement saying that you are not certain whether you will go
- 8   The flowers in the park
- 10   A short question to confirm yes or no from the other party

128

Across

2 A plan
4 Plans for when you are on vacation
7 A short answer to a phone call if the person wanted is not available
8 A table cloth
9 A phrase indicating that (the flight) is via Hong Kong
11 A seat
12 The previous conversation

Down

1 The name of the Chinese school and university winter holiday
3 To calculate
5 To put it on the table
6 To make a long distance call
10 Perfumes

129

Across

2 A word for the time around breakfast
4 To enter through the door
6 Phrase for a soccer match
9 A team which represents the country
10 A general term for people working for an organization
12 People

Down

1 The gates on the soccer ground
3 The first half of a match
5 A phrase indicating the player who scored
7 Half
8 A race
11 Workers

130

Across

4 A statement saying that every year it snows in the winter
7 A cloudy day
8 A short question asking 'how long'
11 The timetable for next week

Down

1 The year just passed
2 The season between spring and autumn
3 Heavy snow
5 An instruction telling somebody to take one tablet every hour
6 A rainy day
9 Unecessary or superfluous
10 To have a lesson
12 To perform

131

			1			2		
			4			6		
		3			5			
				8				
	7						10	
					9			
		11						
			12					

Across
- 3   A watermelon
- 5   Interesting
- 7   A statement saying that poets climb the Great Wall
- 9   The centre of a city
- 11 High mountains
- 12 The top floor

Down
- 1   A cucumber
- 2   Willingness
- 4   Westerners
- 6   Some of the cities
- 8   To climb up to the top of a mountain
- 10 The time around lunch

132

Across
1 Mineral water
4 A statement saying that the income of the middle aged people is low
6 A New Year
7 A common wish when you see somebody off for a trip
9 A short form for science and technology
10 To write letters
11 A short phrase to ask your guests to come frequently when you see them off at the door

Down
2 A statement saying that the level is low
3 A statement saying that every year there is a new technique
5 To receive a letter
8 Very common

133

Across

3 To use a computer to write article
6 To raise or enhance, increase or improve
8 A statement saying that two pieces of bread have already been prepared
11 People who do the service jobs in restaurants or shops
12 People who do manual work in factories

Down

1 The organ in the body that controls thought
2 The main printed part of a book that is studied or read
4 To use silk to make clothes
5 To write postcards
7 A word for handbags
9 Two employees
10 Long thin strips made of flour and water and eaten with sauces

134

Across

4 A statement saying that you are interested in travelling
8 A question asking how many bags there are
9 Understanding (sharing the same character with 7 Down but with different pronunciation)
10 A phrase used when people leave each other
11 Face to face talks

Down

1 The negative answer to the question 'Is it correct?'
2 A person who shows others around tourist sights
3 To be happy
5 A question asking at what time we are meeting
6 Small bag used for travelling
7 To have a cold
12 To talk

135

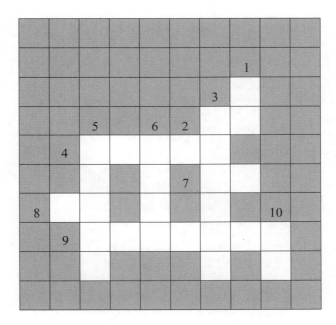

Across

2 Summer
4 To chat with friends
7 Climate
8 Small things
9 A statement saying that you can take a taxi once you are out of the house

Down

1 The word for "four seasons"
3 A statement saying that the temperature is high in the summer
5 To go on a business trip with colleagues
6 Friendly countries
10 Indeed

136

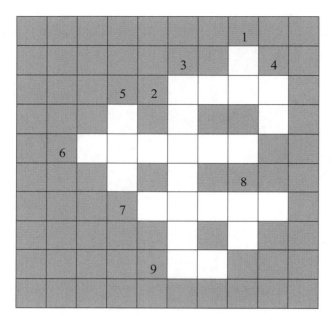

Across

2 A statement saying that he is riding a horse
6 A statement saying that she uses her left hand to write
7 A statement saying that she was run over and injured
9 A phrase mearning to understand or comprehend (sharing the same character with 3 Down but with different pronunciation)

Down

1 Sitting
3 A statement saying that his mobile phone was stolen (sharing the same character with 9 Across but with different pronunciation)
4 Immediately
5 A reply to 'thank you'
8 A word for injured people

137

Across
1 The same currency used in Europe by 12 countries
3 The name of the continent where China is located
6 A statement saying that a bicycle was borrowed
8 To read books
9 A question to find out how many people there are all together
11 A place where you can stop and leave a vehicle for a period of time

Down
2 A statement saying that there are few travel groups to Europe
4 A short statement used to indicate something is ready or finished
5 Five buses
7 Library card
10 The word for a group of people in general

138

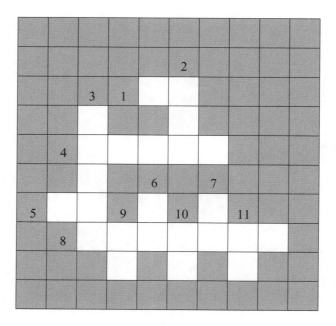

Across

1 For the reason that
4 A question asking how the situation is
5 Very good
8 A statement saying that the office building is in the city centre

Down

2 A short question asking why
3 A statement saying that things are not easy to handle
6 Big building
7 A large important town
9 A public garden or area of ground for public use
10 At home
11 In the middle

139

Across

1 A phrase for half
3 Markets that open in the evening
4 A compliment saying that it is extraordinary, outstanding
6 People with whom one works in the same organization
8 To chat
9 Literature
11 A phrase for changes in the climate
13 A word for being enthusiastic

Down

2 A statement saying to get up at midnight
5 A statement saying to find out about the weather situation
7 Students who study together
10 Culture
12 To change

140

Across
2 To know
3 To read a menu
5 A phrase to indicate 'temperature' using two opposite adjectives
8 A phase for the police office in the busy city center area
11 To use a car
12 A card you send to someone for a celebration

Down
1 A notice written on a piece of paper
4 To watch the excitement/fun
6 A question to find out whose credit card it is
7 The toilet
9 Markets
10 A car you can hire with a driver

What is HSK?

A: Do you know anything about HSK?

B: Yes, HSK stands for hànyǔ shuǐpíng kǎoshì (汉语水平考试, Chinese Proficiency Level Test) and is the world's most well-known test of Chinese language proficiency for non-native speakers. It is similar to TOEFL and IELTS for English language.

TOEFL

HSK

Solutions

1

Across

2. 我们
   wǒ men

4. 你好吗
   nǐ hǎo ma

Down

1. 你们
   nǐ men

3. 我很好
   wǒ hěn hǎo

5. 你呢
   nǐ ne

2

Across

2. 对不起
   duì bu qǐ

Down

1. 一起
   yì qǐ

3. 不客气
   bu kè qì

3

Across

4. 十三日
   shí sān rì

5. 你几岁
   nǐ jǐ suì

6. 老朋友
   lǎo péng you

Down

1. 星期三
   xīng qī sān

2. 十八岁
   shí bā suì

3. 日语老师
   rì yǔ lǎo shī

4

Across

3. 他是我弟弟
   tā shì wǒ dì di

4. 她没有儿子
   tā méi yǒu ér zi

Down

1. 这是你女儿吗
   zhè shì nǐ nǚ ér ma

2. 三弟
   sān dì

4. 没关系
   méi guān xi

5

Across

3. 你喝咖啡吗
   nǐ hē kā fēi ma

4. 红茶
   hóng chá

Down

1. 我也喝绿茶
   wǒ yě hē lǜ chá

2. 你忙吗
   nǐ máng ma

Solutions

6

wǒ mā ma shì lǎo shī
3. 我 妈 妈 是 老 师
dà xué shēng
4. 大 学 生

tā gē ge shì yī shēng
1. 她 哥 哥 是 医 生
lǜ shī
2. 律 师
dà gē
5. 大 哥

7

wǒ gē ge shì dài fu
2. 我 哥 哥 是 大 夫
zhōng guó péng you
3. 中 国 朋 友

nǐ shì nǎ guó rén
1. 你 是 哪 国 人

8

nǐ mèi mei zuò shěn me
4. 你 妹 妹 做 什 么
chī fàn
6. 吃 饭

wǒ mā xǐ huan zuò zhōng guó fàn
1. 我 妈 喜 欢 做 中 国 饭
jiě mèi
2. 姐 妹
zěn me yàng
3. 怎 么 样
nǐ ne
5. 你 呢

9

hěn gāo xìng rèn shi nín
2. 很 高 兴 认 识 您
nǐ hǎo
4. 你 好
nǐ péng you xìng shén me
6. 你 朋 友 姓 什 么

wǒ hěn hǎo
1. 我 很 好
nín guì xìng
3. 您 贵 姓
nǐ men
5. 你 们
nǐ zǎo
7. 你 早

10

yīng yǔ shū
2. 英 语 书
měi guó
5. 美 国

Solutions

fáng zi
6. 房子
fàn guǎn
7. 饭馆

Down
xué hàn yǔ
1. 学汉语
yīng guó fàn
3. 英国饭
shū fáng
4. 书房

11

Across
nǐ jīn nián duō dà
2. 你今年多大
jiā li rén
6. 家里人
liù yuè yī hào
7. 六月一号

Down
hòu nián
1. 后年
jīn tiān jǐ hào
3. 今天几号
dà jiā hǎo
4. 大家好
dà rén
5. 大人

12

Across
jīn nián
1. 今年

nǐ men máng bu máng
4. 你们忙不忙
tiān qì hǎo ma
5. 天气好吗

Down
jīn tiān bù lěng
2. 今天不冷
wǒ men dōu hěn hǎo
3. 我们都很好

13

Across
jīn wǎn
2. 今晚
shàng ge yuè
4. 上个月
xiàng zài jǐ diǎn zhōng
5. 现在几点钟

Down
shí èr yuè
1. 十二月
wǎn shàng qī diǎn sān kè
3. 晚上七点三刻
zài jiā
6. 在家

14

Across
tā shì bu shì běi jīng rén
3. 他是不是北京人
wǒ men
5. 我们
xiǎo zhāng
6. 小张

Solutions

jiě jie
7. 姐姐

Down

zhè shì wáng xiǎo jie
1. 这 是 王 小 姐
ài rén
2. 爱人
tā men
4. 他们

15

Across

wǎn fàn
1. 晚饭
wǒ men wǔ diǎn bàn jiàn
5. 我们 五点 半见
xīng qī rì
7. 星期日

Down

wǎn shang shí èr diǎn
2. 晚 上 十二点
tā men
3. 她们
zài jiàn
4. 再见
wǔ yuè yī rì
6. 五月一日

16

Across

míng tiān nǐ yǒu shí jiān ma
3. 明天你有时间吗
wǔ fàn
4. 午饭

Down

shén me shí hou
1. 什么时候
jīn tiān xià wǔ
2. 今天下午

17

Across

jīn tiān wǒ qǐng kè
2. 今天我请客
hòu nián
5. 后年
yǒu shí hou
6. 有时候
zuò yè
7. 作业

Down

qián tiān
1. 前天
jīn nián
3. 今年
wǒ méi you gōng zuò
4. 我没有工作

18

Across

níng guì xìng
2. 您贵姓
zhōng wén
4. 中文
wài guó
5. 外国
nǐ máng ma
6. 你忙吗

Solutions

Down

wǒ xìng wáng zhāng
1. 我 姓 王／张

nín shì zhōng guó rén ma
3. 您 是 中 国 人 吗

19

Across

zhè shì wǒ de míng piàn
2. 这 是 我 的 名 片

xià wǔ
5. 下 午

Down

hǎo de
1. 好 的

wǒ lái jiè shào yí xià
3. 我 来 介 绍 一 下

míng zi
4. 名 字

20

Across

zhōng wén diàn yǐng
2. 中 文 电 影

hē bu hē chá
6. 喝 不 喝 茶

Down

yīng wén
1. 英 文

zhōng guó chá
3. 中 国 茶

diàn shì
4. 电 视

duì bu qǐ
5. 对 不 起

21

Across

wǒ zhōu mò cháng cháng kàn
3. 我 周 末 常 常 看

diàn shì
电 视

qiú yǒu
6. 球 友

lǐ xiao jie
7. 李 小 姐

Down

tā xǐ huan kàn shū
1. 她 喜 欢 看 书

lǎo zhōu
2. 老 周

wǒ péng you xìng lǐ
4. 我 朋 友 姓 李

cháng huí jiā
5. 常 回 家

22

Across

jīn tiān xīng qī jǐ
3. 今 天 星 期 几

xīn nián
7. 新 年

kǒu yǔ kè
8. 口 语 课

rì běn rén
9. 日 本 人

Solutions

Down

qián tiān
1. 前 天

rì qī
2. 日 期

jīn nián
4. 今 年

xīng qī rì
5. 星 期 日

jǐ kǒu rén
6. 几 口 人

běn zi
10. 本 子

23

Across

wǒ lái jiè shào yí xià
3. 我 来 介 绍 一 下

shì ma
4. 是 吗

kě yǐ ma
5. 可 以 吗

Down

xiǎo wáng lái le ma
1. 小 王 来 了 吗

gěi wǒ yì bēi kě lè ba
2. 给 我 一 杯 可 乐 吧

24

Across

lǎo wáng
1. 老 王

tài hǎo le
3. 太 好 了

duì bu qī
4. 对 不 起

hěn hǎo chī
5. 很 好 吃

kàn péng you
6. 看 朋 友

yīng yǔ shū
8. 英 语 书

dé guó
9. 德 国

cài dān
10. 菜 单

Down

wáng tài tai bù xǐ huan chī
2. 王 太 太 不 喜 欢 吃

yīng guó cài
英 国 菜

kàn shū
7. 看 书

25

Across

nǐ hē shuǐ hái shì hē jiǔ
3. 你 喝 水 还 是 喝 酒

chī fàn
5. 吃 饭

zhōng wén shū diàn
6. 中 文 书 店

Down

lěng shuǐ
1. 冷 水

zhè shì bù shì nǐ de shū
2. 这 是 不 是 你 的 书

nǐ xiǎng chī shén me
4. 你 想 吃 什 么

Solutions

26

Across

1. 好 吗
   hǎo ma

5. 你 想 不 想 去 打 球
   nǐ xiǎng bu xiǎng qù dǎ qiú

7. 请 看 一 下
   qǐng kàn yí xia

8. 什 么
   shén me

Down

2. 好 久 不 见
   hǎo jiǔ bú jiàn

3. 他 去 不 去 看 电 影
   tā qù bu qù kàn diàn yǐng

4. 足 球
   zú qiú

5. 你 觉 得 怎 么 样
   nǐ jué de zěn me yàng

27

Across

3. 你 们 大 学 有 几 个 系
   nǐ men dà xué yǒu jǐ ge xì

Down

1. 你 有 没 有 姐 姐
   nǐ yǒu mei you jiě jie

2. 六 个 外 国 人
   liù ge wài guó rén

4. 大 学 生
   dà xué shēng

28

Across

1. 今 年
   jīn nián

5. 明 天
   míng tiān

6. 你 的 生 日 是 几 月 几 号
   nǐ de shēng rì shì jǐ yuè jǐ hào

Down

2. 今 天 星 期 几
   jīn tiān xīng qī jǐ

3. 这 是 谁 的 书
   zhè shì shuí de shū

4. 祝 你 生 日 快 乐
   zhù nǐ shēng rì kuài lè

7. 有 几 个 学 生
   yǒu jǐ ge xué shēng

29

Across

3. 你 在 哪 儿 工 作
   nǐ zài nǎ r gōng zuò

5. 书 店
   shū diàn

6. 饭 馆
   fàn guǎn

7. 学 校
   xué xiào

Down

1. 她 喜 欢 在 图 书 馆 学 习
   tā xǐ huan zài tú shū guǎn xué xí

Solutions

2. 聊天儿
liáo tiān r

4. 工人
gōng rén

30

Across

1. 星期一
xīng qī yī

3. 昨天
zuó tiān

5. 我在商场买酒
wǒ zài shāng chǎng mǎi jiǔ

7. 大家好
dà jiā hǎo

Down

2. 星期天你在不在家
xīng qī tiān nǐ zài bu zài jiā

4. 葡萄酒
pú tao jiǔ

6. 买东西
mǎi dōng xi

31

Across

3. 一斤苹果多少钱
yì jīn píng guǒ duō shǒo qián

5. 您贵姓
nín guì xìng

Down

1. 水果太贵
shuǐ guǒ tài guì

2. 有钱人
yǒu qián rén

4. 一共八块五
yí gòng bā kuài wǔ

32

Across

1. 你早
nǐ zǎo

3. 今天几点吃晚饭
jīn tiān jǐ diǎn chī wǎn fàn

Down

2. 早上八点上课
zǎo shang bā diǎn shàng kè

4. 今年
jīn nián

5. 饭馆
fàn guǎn

33

Across

3. 我会说法语
wǒ huì shuō fǎ yǔ

6. 老人
lǎo rén

7. 学习
xué xí

8. 语法
yǔ fǎ

Down

1. 不会
bú huì

2. 德语老师
dé yǔ lǎo shī

4. 我想学汉语
wǒ xiǎng xué hàn yǔ

Solutions

shuō huà
5. 说 话

34

Across

qǐng wèn wáng lǎo shī zài ma
3. 请 问 王 老 师 在 吗
gōng gòng qì chē
5. 公 共 汽 车
jiào shì
6. 教 室

Down

lǐ lù shī bàn gàong shi
1. 李 律 师 办 公 室
yǒu shì ma
2. 有 事 么
qìng jìn
4. 请 进

35

Across

míng tiān wǒ bù néng lái shàng kè
3. 明 天 我 不 能 来 上 课

Down

xué hàn yǔ bù róng yì
1. 学 汉 语 不 容 易
tā yīng gāi lái
2. 他 应 该 来
míng nián
4. 明 年

36

Across

xiǎo wáng jīn nián sān shí wǔ suì
4. 小 王 今 年 三 十 五 岁
dà xué
8. 大 学
shí yuè yī rì
10. 十 月 一 日
xīng qī tiān
11. 星 期 天

Down

nǐ jǐ suì
1. 你 几 岁
lǎo wáng
2. 老 王
míng nián
3. 明 年
xiǎo xué
5. 小 学
jīn tiān
6. 今 天
sān bǎi liù shí wǔ tiān
7. 三 百 六 十 五 天
shēng rì
9. 生 日

37

Across

jīn tiān xià wǔ wǒ yào kāi huì
4. 今 天 下 午 我 要 开 会
chá guǎn
9. 茶 馆

Down

xīng qī tiān
1. 星 期 天

Solutions

zhōng wǔ
2. 中 午

wǔ huì
3. 舞 会

jīn wǎn
5. 今 晚

xià xīng qī
6. 下 星 期

wǒ qǐng nǐ hē chá
7. 我 请 你 喝 茶

kāi qì chē
8. 开 汽 车

38

tā yào qù yī yuàn kàn bìng
4. 他 要 去 医 院 看 病

liǎng píng kě lè
6. 两 瓶 可 乐

wǒ yào yì píng pí jiǔ
1. 我 要 一 瓶 啤 酒

zhōng yī
2. 中 医

shēng bìng
3. 生 病

kàn shū
5. 看 书

39

zuó tiān
2. 昨 天

wài yǔ wén
3. 外 语 / 文

nǐ jiā yǒu jǐ kǒu rén
6. 你 家 有 几 口 人

jīn tiān xīng qī jǐ
1. 今 天 星 期 几

wài guó rén
4. 外 国 人

wáng jiā
5. 王 家

yǒu zhōng guó chá ma
7. 有 中 国 茶 吗

kǒu yǔ kè
8. 口 语 课

40

dà ren
2. 大 人

míng tiān nǐ yǒu shí jiān ma
5. 明 天 你 有 时 间 吗

liǎng wèi
7. 两 位

nǐ shén me shí hou yǒu kòng
1. 你 什 么 时 候 有 空

dà rè tiān
3. 大 热 天

xíng ma
4. 行 吗

nǐ shì nǎ wèi
2. 你 是 哪 位

Solutions

41

Across

4. nǐ huì shuō shàng hǎi huà ma
   你 会 说 上 海 话 吗
7. yǔ fǎ shū
   语 法 书
9. lǎo péng you
   老 朋 友

Down

1. pǔ tōng huà
   普 通 话
2. bú huì
   不 会
3. zǎo shang
   早 上
5. nǐ qǐng zuò
   你 请 坐
6. shuō hàn yǔ
   说 汉 语
8. fǎ wén / yǔ lǎo shī
   法 文 / 语 老 师

42

Across

3. wáng lǎo shī qǐng tā tīng yīn yuè
   王 老 师 请 她 听 音 乐
5. nǐ bié dǎ qiú
   你 别 打 球
7. fàn qián
   饭 前

Down

1. wǒ qǐng xiǎo wáng dǎ diàn huà
   我 请 小 王 打 电 话

(43 top)

2. fā yīn
   发 音
4. tīng lù yīn
   听 录 音
6. nǐ dě chī fàn
   你 得 吃 饭

43

Across

2. tā shì shuí
   他 是 谁
4. nǐ měi tiān jǐ diǎn qǐ chuáng
   你 每 天 几 点 起 床
7. zú qiú
   足 球

Down

1. nǐ gēn shuí yì qǐ qù dǎ qiú
   你 跟 谁 一 起 去 打 球
3. qián tiān
   前 天
5. měi ge xīng qī
   每 个 星 期
6. jǐ wèi
   几 位

44

Across

2. zǎo fàn
   早 饭
4. jīn tiān wǎn shang
   今 天 晚 上
7. qù nián
   去 年

Solutions

Down

1. 雨天
   (yǔ tiān)
2. 早 上
   (zǎo shang)
5. 今 年
   (jīn nián)
6. 晚 安
   (wǎn ān)

45

Across

2. 用 中 英 文
   (yòng zhōng yīng wén)
5. 不 谢
   (bú xiè)
6. 她 的 字 写 得 很 好
   (tā de zì xiě de hěn hǎo)
7. 复 习
   (fù xí)
8. 好 多 人
   (hǎo duō rén)

Down

1. 你 的 英 语 说 得 真 好
   (nǐ de yīng yǔ shuō de zhēn hǎo)
3. 好 不 好
   (hǎo bu hǎo)
4. 汉 字 练 习
   (hàn zì liàn xí)

46

Across

4. 我 租 了 一 间 房 子
   (wǒ zū le yì jiān fáng zi)

5. 火 车 站
   (huǒ chē zhàn)

Down

1. 出 租 汽 车
   (chū zū qì chē)
2. 看 一 下
   (kán yí xia)
3. 厨 房
   (chú fáng)

47

Across

4. 你 买 什 么
   (nǐ mǎi shén me)
5. 你 好
   (nǐ hǎo)
6. 看 书
   (kàn shū)
8. 瓶 子
   (píng zi)
9. 法 国 酒
   (fǎ guó jiǔ)

Down

1. 为 什 么
   (wèi shén me)
2. 我 买 一 瓶 酒
   (wǒ mǎi yì píng jiǔ)
3. 很 好 看
   (hěn hǎo kàn)
7. 书 法
   (shū fǎ)
10. 国 家
    (guó jiā)

Solutions

48

Across

2. qīng kè
请客

4. tā bā diǎn bàn cái lái
他八点半才来

6. méi yǒu
没有

8. jiā li rén
家里人

9. wán r
玩儿

Down

1. wǒ sì diǎn jiù huí jiā le
我四点就回家了

3. qīng jìn lai ba
请进来吧

5. tā yǒu yì diǎn r máng
他有一点儿忙

7. hǎo rén
好人

49

Across

4. lǎo wáng qǐng wǒ meng qù tā jiā
老王请我们去他家

hē chá
喝茶

6. pǔ tōng huà
普通话

Down

1. wǒ méi gěi tā dǎ diàn huà
我没给他打电话

2. shù xué lǎo shī
数学老师

3. nǐ hē shén me
你喝什么

5. qǐng wèn
请问

50

Across

2. xué xiào
学校

3. zhè shì lǐ xiān sheng
这是李先生

6. dé yǔ shū
德语书

8. shuí shì zhāng huá
谁是张华

9. bǐ shì wǒ de
笔是我的

Down

1. xiǎo xué shēng
小学生

4. zhè běn shū shì shuí de
这本书是谁的

5. lǐ lǎo shi
李老师

7. lǎo huá qiáo
老华侨

51

Across

2. wǒ bù hē jiǔ
我不喝酒

6. nǐ zěn me méi qù kàn diàn yǐng
你怎么没去看电影

Solutions

chàng gē
8. 唱 歌

Down

nǐ xiǎng hē shén me
1. 你 想 喝 什 么

wǒ gēn nǐ yì qǐ chàng
3. 我 跟 你 一 起 唱

huí qù
4. 回 去

dǎ diàn huà
5. 打 电 话

méi wèn tí
7. 没 问 题

52

Across

zhè shì shén me yú
3. 这 是 什 么 鱼

Down

wèi shén me
1. 为 什 么

tā shì shuí
2. 她 是 谁

yú tāng
4. 鱼 汤

53

Across

dōng tiān
2. 冬 天

tīng shuō
4. 听 说

kè wén
5. 课 文

xiǎo wáng zěn me méi yǒu lái
7. 小 王 怎 么 没 有 来

huí qù
10. 回 去

Down

zuó tiān de kè hěn yǒu yì si
1. 昨 天 的 课 很 有 意 思

nǐ shuō shén me
3. 你 说 什 么

guó wáng
6. 国 王

xiǎo jie
8. 小 姐

zěn me huí shì
9. 怎 么 回 事

54

Across

tā cháng qù zhōng guó
4. 他 常 去 中 国

měi nián
5. 每 年

lǎo shī jiāo wǒ men xiě zì
6. 老 师 教 我 们 写 字

bǐ jì
8. 笔 记

Down

tā zài zhōng xué jiāo hàn yǔ
1. 他 在 中 学 教 汉 语

jīng cháng
2. 经 常

tā měi tiān xiě rì jì
3. 她 每 天 写 日 记

lǎo tóng xué
7. 老 同 学

Solutions

55

Across

2. 问题
   wèn tí

5. 回答
   huí dá

7. 她 会 用 中 文 写 信
   tā huì yòng zhōng wén xiě xìn

10. 听 说
    tīng shuō

Down

1. 意 大 利 文
   yì dà lì wén

3. 问 答
   wèn dá

4. 不 用 谢
   bú yòng xiè

6. 回 信
   huí xìn

8. 她 不 说 日 语
   tā bú shuō rì yǔ

9. 写 字 练 习
   xiě zì liàn xí

56

Across

3. 这 个 笔 太 贵 了
   zhè ge bǐ tài guì le

5. 王 教 授
   wáng jiào shòu

6. 生 日
   shēng rì

Down

1. 毛 笔
   máo bǐ

2. 您 贵 姓
   nín guì xìng

4. 这 是 王 先 生
   zhè shì wáng xiān sheng

57

Across

3. 我 得 走 了
   wǒ děi zǒu le

5. 吃 了 饭 以 后 就 看 电 视
   chī le fàn yǐ hòu jiù kàn diàn shì

8. 作 业
   zuò yè

Down

1. 她 得 用 电 脑 工 作
   tā děi yòng diàn nǎo gōng zuò

2. 你 看 了 吗
   nǐ kàn le ma

4. 最 后
   zuì hòu

6. 以 前
   yǐ qián

7. 就 来 了
   jiù lái le

58

Across

2. 电 话
   diàn huà

4. 收 音 机
   shōu yīn jī

Solutions

Down

1. guǎng dōng huà
广 东 话

3. diàn shì jī
电 视 机

5. yīn yuè
音 乐

59

Across

4. yǒu mei you chá
有 没 有 茶

5. zhōng guó rén
中 国 人

6. fǎ wén
法 文

7. tā nǚ péng you zuò shén me
他 女 朋 友 做 什 么
gōng zuò
工 作

Down

1. tā de zhōng wén zěn me yàng
他 的 中 文 怎 么 样

2. tā yǒu liǎng ge nǚ er
她 有 两 个 女 儿

3. hóng chá
红 茶

8. zuò dàn gāo
做 蛋 糕

60

Across

2. xiǎo lǐ bú zài jiào shì
小 李 不 在 教 室

4. nà shì shén me
那 是 什 么

7. xiě xìn
写 信

8. nǐ yù xí le ma
你 预 习 了 吗

Down

1. tā jiāo wǒ zěn me xiě hàn zì
她 教 我 怎 么 写 汉 字

3. dàn kě shì
但 / 可 是

5. nà tài hǎo le
那 太 好 了

6. tiān qì yù bào
天 气 预 报

61

Across

3. xiǎo wáng jīn nián shí liù suì
小 王 今 年 十 六 岁

7. jiě jie
姐 姐

8. wǎn shang
晚 上

10. rì běn
日 本

12. zuò fàn
做 饭

Down

1. xīng qī liù
星 期 六

2. qù nián
去 年

4. xiǎo jie
小 姐

Solutions

jīn tiān zǎo shàng
5. 今天早上

shí yuè yī rì
6. 十月一日

wǎn fàn
9. 晚饭

běn zi
11. 本子

62

Across
nǐ huì bu huì xiě hàn zì
4. 你会不会写汉字

yīng yǔ kè běn
6. 英语课本

Down
tā huì shuō dé yǔ
1. 她会说德语

wǒ huì zuò rì běn fàn
2. 我会做日本饭

míng zi
3. 名字

hàn yǔ
5. 汉语

63

Across
shì bu shì
3. 是不是

wǎn shàng
4. 晚上

wǔ fàn
6. 午饭

qǐng kè
7. 请客

tā gěi le wǒ yì zhāng zhào piàn
9. 她给了我一张照片

Down
zhè shì wǒ de míng piàn
1. 这是我的名片

zǎo shang
2. 早上

wǎn fàn hǎo le ma
5. 晚饭好了吗

qǐng děng yí xià
8. 请等一下

zhào xiàng jī
10. 照相机

64

Across
píng guǒ zěn me mài
3. 苹果怎么卖

bào zhǐ
6. 报纸

yí yàng
7. 一样

Down
nà shì shén me
1. 那是什么

shuǐ guǒ
2. 水果

zěn me yàng
4. 怎么样

mài bào de
5. 卖报的

yì fēn qián
8. 一分钱

Solutions

65

míng zi
10. 名字

Across

shàng yīng yǔ kè
2. 上英语课

shuí huì dǎ wǎng qiú
5. 谁会打网球

duì yǒu
9. 队友

míng tiān jiàn
10. 明天见

Down

xī bān yá yǔ
2. 西班牙语

xué sheng men
3. 学生们

xué xí xiě hàn zì
4. 学习写汉字

zài xué xiào
6. 在学校

nǚ péng you
8. 女朋友

Down

kǒu yǔ
1. 口语

yīng tè wǎng
3. 英特网

kāi huì
4. 开会

shuí shì lǐ míng
6. 谁是李明

dǎ zì
7. 打字

qiú duì
8. 球队

67

Across

wǔ fàn chī shén me
2. 午饭吃什么

bú yòng chī yào
5. 不用吃药

wǒ péng you shì gōng sī jīng lǐ
6. 我朋友是公司经理

dōng xī
8. 东西

66

Across

mǎi dōng xi
1. 买东西

tā men zài liàn xí shuō hàn yǔ
5. 他们在练习说汉语

nǚ xiào
7. 女校

hàn yīng cí diǎn
9. 汉英词典

Down

shàng wǔ
1. 上午

chī zhōng yào hái shì chī xī yào
3. 吃中药还是吃西药

zhè bú shì wǒ de
4. 这不是我的

jīng jì
7. 经济

Solutions

68

Across

3. tiān tiān wǎn shàng
   天 天 晚 上
6. wǔ fàn
   午 饭

Down

1. míng tiān
   明 天
2. jīn wǎn
   今 晚
4. tiān qì
   天 气
5. shàng wǔ
   上 午
6. fàn zhuō
   饭 桌

69

Across

1. yīng guó nǚ wáng
   英 国 女 王
5. wǒ qù péng you jiā wán r
   我 去 朋 友 家 玩 儿
8. dà ér zi
   大 儿 子
10. dà nǎo
    大 脑
12. shàng yī
    上 衣

Down

2. wáng lǎo shī jiā
   王 老 师 家

3. liáo tiān r
   聊 天 儿
4. nǐ qù nǎ r
   你 去 哪 儿
6. yǒu hǎo
   友 好
7. wán diàn nǎo
   玩 电 脑
9. dà yī
   大 衣
11. dà yǔ
    大 雨

70

Across

2. wǒ bú huì hē jiǔ
   我 不 会 喝 酒
4. duō xiè
   多 谢
6. qián bu gòu
   钱 不 够

Down

1. qǐng hē chá
   请 喝 茶
3. bú yòng xiè
   不 用 谢
5. duō shao qián
   多 少 钱

71

Across

3. tā cháng bāng wǒ liàn xí kǒu yǔ
   他 常 帮 我 练 习 口 语
6. nǐ men hē le shén me jiǔ
   你 们 喝 了 什 么 酒

Solutions

qiān bǐ
7. 铅笔

Down

tā gěi wǒ mǎi le yì zhī bǐ
1. 他给我买了一支笔
nǐ xué xí shén me zhuān yè
2. 你学习什么专业
tā shì nǐ gē ge ma
4. 他是你哥哥吗
yǔ fǎ
5. 语法

72

Across

nǐ ne
1. 你呢
dōng nán
3. 东南
tā zhèn zài gēn lǎo shī shuō huà
7. 他正在跟老师说话
qǐng jìn lai
8. 请进来
gōng yuán
9. 公园
wò shì
10. 卧室

Down

nǐ wèn tā ba
2. 你问他吧
nán jīng huà
4. 南京话
qǐng gēn wǒ lái
5. 请跟我来
lù shī bàn gōng shì
6. 律师办公室

73

Across

shǒu biǎo
3. 手表
tā xìng shén me
4. 她姓什么
zǒng shì
6. 总是
tài jí quán
7. 太极拳

Down

nǐ de shǒu zěn me le
1. 你的手怎么了
nín guì xìng
2. 您贵姓
tā shì lǐ tài tài
5. 她是李太太

74

Across

nín zǎo
1. 您早
wǒ lái wǎn le
3. 我来晚了
nián qīng rén yīng yǔ shuō de
7. 年轻人英语说得
hěn liú lì
很流利
hǎo jiǔ bú jiàn
8. 好久不见

Down

nín duō dà nián jì le
2. 您多大年纪了

Solutions

wǎn shàng shuì de hǎo bù hǎo
4. 晚 上 睡得好不好
wài guó rén
5. 外 国 人
rì yǔ bù hǎo xué
6. 日 语 不 好 学

75

Across
nǐ kě yǐ yòng diàn nǎo zuò
5. 你可以用电脑做
gōng kè
功 课
kě shì
7. 可 是
kuài lè
8. 快 乐
hǎo ma
9. 好 吗

Down
lù yīn diàn huà
1. 录 音 电 话
yīn yuè kè
2. 音 乐 课
suǒ yǐ
3. 所 以
fàn zuò hǎo le ma
4. 饭 做 好 了 吗
kě kǒu kě lè
6. 可 口 可 乐
hǎo péng you
10. 好 朋 友

76

Across
yīn wei
1. 因 为
shén me
3. 什 么
zěn me
4. 怎 么
yí yàng
6. 一 样

Down
wèi shén me
2. 为 什 么
zěn yàng
5. 怎 样
yí dìng
6. 一 定

77

Across
tā zhù zài yīng guó de běi bù
2. 他 住 在 英 国 的 北 部
shàng hǎi rén shuō pǔ tōng huà ma
5. 上 海 人 说 普 通 话 吗
hàn yǔ yǔ fǎ hěn róng yì
6. 汉 语 语 法 很 容 易

Down
tā yīng yǔ shuō de hěn liú li
1. 她 英 语 说 得 很 流 利
tā bú shàng kǒu yǔ kè
3. 他 不 上 口 语 课
běi jīng huà
4. 北 京 话

Solutions

78

Across

2. yīn yuè huì
音乐会

4. shàng ge yuè
上个月

5. kě ài de
可爱的

7. zhù nǐ shēng rì kuài lè
祝你生日快乐

11. fù xí
复习

Down

1. zài huì shang
在会上

3. bā yuè yī rì
八月一日

6. kě lè
可乐

8. zhù xué xí hǎo
祝学习好

9. shēng cí
生词

10. kuài chē
快车

79

Across

2. tā men
他们

4. yào shi
要是

6. bù zhǔn chōu yān
不准抽烟

7. yì qǐ
一起

Down

1. wǒ men
我们

3. tā shì mài yān de
他是卖烟的

5. duì bu qǐ
对不起

8. yì diǎn r
一点儿

80

Across

2. lǎo shī jiā
老师家

3. shū fǎ
书法

4. shāng diàn
商店

8. tā gāng cóng zhōng guó huí
他刚从中国回
měi guó
美国

9. zhēn duì bu qǐ
真对不起

Down

1. zhè jiā shū diàn de zhōng wén shū
这家书店的中文书
bù duō
不多

5. wǒ děi huí jiā
我得回家

6. wǒ gāng lái
我刚来

Solutions

měi guó
7. 美 国

81

Across

xiǎng fa
2. 想 法
wǒ xiǎng mǎi yí jiàn chèn shān
5. 我 想 买 一 件 衬 衫
fú wù shēng
8. 服 务 生
zhǎo nín wǔ kuài liù máo qī
9. 找 您 五 块 六 毛 七

Down

wǒ xiǎng yi xiǎng
1. 我 想 一 想
yùn dòng shān
3. 运 动 衫
liǎng jiàn yī fu
4. 两 件 衣 服
wǒ gěi nǐ zhǎo zhao
6. 我 给 你 找 找
mǎi dōng xi
7. 买 东 西

82

Across

nǐ huì xiě hàn zì ma
3. 你 会 写 汉 字 吗
kè běn
6. 课 本
xué xí
8. 学 习
lái yì tiáo yú
10. 来 一 条 鱼

Down

tīng xiě
1. 听 写
míng zi
2. 名 字
huì huà liàn xí
4. 会 话 练 习
hàn yǔ kè
5. 汉 语 课
běn lái
7. 本 来
xué xiào
9. 学 校

83

Across

bú yòng pái duì
2. 不 用 排 队
lái měi guó liú xué de rén hěn duō
5. 来 美 国 留 学 的 人 很 多
nǐ nín zǎo
9. 你 / 您 早
guǎng dōng huà
10. 广 东 话

Down

zú qiú duì
1. 足 球 队
bú yòng xué xí pǔ tōng huà
3. 不 用 学 习 普 通 话
zhōng guó yín háng
4. 中 国 银 行
lái de zǎo
6. 来 得 早
rén mín bì
7. 人 民 币

Solutions

duō xiè
8. 多 谢

nǐ lèi ma
7. 你 累 吗

84

Across

xué sheng
2. 学 生

měi ge xīng qī
4. 每 个 星 期

kù zi wǔ shí sān kuài
6. 裤 子 五 十 三 块

bàn xiǎo shí
7. 半 小 时

shuāng rén chuáng
10. 双 人 床

Down

tā měi tiān wǔ diǎn bàn qǐ chuáng
1. 她 每 天 五 点 半 起 床

xué qī
3. 学 期

cháng kù
5. 长 裤

shí jiān
8. 时 间

liǎng shuāng xié
9. 两 双 鞋

85

Across

tā zuò de gōng zuò hěn nán
3. 他 做 的 工 作 很 难

wài guó
5. 外 国

fàn guǎn
6. 饭 馆

Down

nǐ huì zuò zhōng guó fàn ma
1. 你 会 做 中 国 饭 吗

wǒ hěn hǎo
2. 我 很 好

gōng rén
4. 工 人

86

Across

bú kè qí
2. 不 客 气

zhè ge tú shū guǎn zhēn dà
6. 这 个 图 书 馆 真 大

xiǎo shí
9. 小 时

kàn diàn yǐng
10. 看 电 影

Down

tiān qì
1. 天 气

bú tài dà
3. 不 太 大

měi gè
4. 每 个

huán shū shí jiān
5. 还 书 时 间

zhè me xiǎo
7. 这 么 小

zhēn hǎo kàn
8. 真 好 看

diàn shì
11. 电 视

Solutions

87

Across

1. 不在 *bú zài*

3. 哪里 *nǎ li*

4. 女儿 *nǚ ér*

7. 这是两百块钱 *zhè shì liǎng bǎi kuài qián*

9. 货物 *huò wù*

10. 服务员 *fú wù yuán*

Down

2. 在哪儿付钱 *zài nǎ r fù qián*

5. 谁是售货员 *shuí shì shòu huò yuán*

6. 一百年 *yī bǎi nián*

8. 衣服 *yī fu*

88

Across

2. 我只会说法语 *wǒ zhǐ huì shuō fǎ yǔ*

4. 学习中文 *xué xí zhōng wén*

Down

1. 语法课 *yǔ fǎ kè*

3. 会话练习 *huì huà liàn xí*

5. 学校 *xué xiào*

6. 中学生 *zhōng xué shēng*

89

Across

2. 她爱人 *tā ài rén*

4. 因为 *yīn wei*

6. 您喜欢什么颜色的 *nín xǐ huan shén me yán sè de*

8. 又高又大 *yòu gāo yòu dà*

10. 号码 *hào mǎ*

Down

1. 美人 *měi rén*

3. 她为什么不高兴 *tā wèi shén me bù gāo xìng*

5. 黄色 *huáng sè*

7. 欢乐 *huān lè*

9. 大号 *dà hào*

90

Across

2. 下课 *xià kè*

Solutions

zhōng wǔ
4. 中 午

yīn wei tài nán le
6. 因 为 太 难 了

nà me
8. 那 么

nán kàn
10. 难 看

nǎ r
12. 哪 儿

shū diàn
13. 书 店

Down

shàng kè
1. 上 课

xià wǔ
3. 下 午

zhōng wén nán bu nán
5. 中 文 难 不 难

wèi shén me
7. 为 什 么

nà r
9. 那 儿

kàn shū
11. 看 书

91

Across

kǎo miàn bāo
1. 烤 面 包

wǒ qiú dǎ de hěn hǎo
4. 我 球 打 得 很 好

tā yǒu zhōng wén míng zì
6. 他 有 中 文 名 字

diàn nǎo
9. 电 脑

bú dà
10. 不 大

Down

kǎo yā hěn yǒu míng
2. 烤 鸭 很 有 名

zú qiú
3. 足 球

wǒ gěi tā dǎ diàn huà
5. 我 给 他 打 电 话

wén xué
7. 文 学

zì tài dà
8. 字 太 大

92

Across

wǒ qù zhǎo tā
2. 我 去 找 他

jīng cháng
4. 经 常

wǔ shuì
5. 午 睡

zhè shuāng xié tài dà le
7. 这 双 鞋 太 大 了

xiǎo chuáng
10. 小 床

Down

nǐ qù ba
1. 你 去 吧

tā yǐ jīng shuì jiào le
3. 他 已 经 睡 觉 了

qiú xié
6. 球 鞋

shuāng rén chuáng
8. 双 人 床

Solutions

tài guì le
9. 太 贵 了

93

Across

shàng shān
2. 上 山
dōng nán xī běi
5. 东 南 西 北
fāng xiàng
8. 方 向
huì huà
9. 会 话

Down

wǎn shang
1. 晚 上
shān dōng
3. 山 东
guǎng xī
4. 广 西
nán jīng
6. 南 京
běi fāng huà
7. 北 方 话

94

Across

yǒu hěn duō wèn tí yào wèn
3. 有 很 多 问 题 要 问
yǒu ge shī fu xìng wáng
6. 有 个 师 傅 姓 王
jiāo shū
9. 教 书
xué xí de hǎo dì fang
10. 学 习 的 好 地 方

Down

bù duō
1. 不 多
qǐng wèn
2. 请 问
hěn duō yǒu míng de diàn yǐng
4. 很 多 有 名 的 电 影
wèn lǎo shī
5. 问 老 师
wáng jiào shòu
7. 王 教 授
xiǎo xué
8. 小 学
dì tú
11. 地 图

95

Across

xià cì
3. 下 次
jīn tiān wǒ bù xiǎng qù shàng kè
5. 今 天 我 不 想 去 上 课
lǜ chá
9. 绿 茶
chūn tiān
10. 春 天

Down

nǐ xiǎng yi xiǎng
1. 你 想 一 想
zài fēi jī shang
2. 在 飞 机 上
xià yǔ tiān
4. 下 雨 天
wǒ yào hē chá
6. 我 要 喝 茶

Solutions

qù nián qiū tiān
7. 去年 秋天
kè wài liàn xí
8. 课外 练习

96

Across

lǎo wài
1. 老外
fǎ yǔ
4. 法语
zhōng huá rén mín gòng hé guó
6. 中 华人民 共 和国
tú shū guǎn zài nǎ r
10. 图书 馆 在 哪儿

Down

wài guó rén
2. 外国人
yí gòng
3. 一共
fǎ guó
5. 法国
zhōng guó dì tú
7. 中 国地图
fàn guǎn
8. 饭馆
huā r
9. 花儿
shū diàn
11. 书 店
nǎ li nǎ li
12. 哪里哪里

97

Across

zài jiā shuì le sān tiān
2. 在家 睡了三天
fáng zi li shén me yě méi yǒu
5. 房子里什么也没有
mài wán le
7. 卖 完了
jiè shū
9. 借 书

Down

dì sān kè hái méi xué wán
1. 第三课还没学完
zài gōng yuán li
3. 在 公 园里
shuì de zěn me yàng
4. 睡 得 怎么 样
fáng zū
6. 房租
mài shū
8. 卖书

98

Across

mǎi mai
1. 买卖
nǐ chuān de xié zi duō dà hào
5. 你穿的鞋子多大号
duǎn qún
9. 短 裙
lǎo nián rén
10. 老年人

Down

mài cài de
2. 卖菜的

Solutions

3. 孩子 (hái zi)
4. 几号 (jǐ hào)
6. 穿红裙子的人 (chuān hóng qún zi de rén)
7. 鞋帽店 (xié mào diàn)
8. 大学一年级 (dà xué yī nián jí)

99

Across

4. 上海在中国东部 (shàng hǎi zài zhōng guó dōng bù)
8. 大学 (dà xué)
10. 旁边 (páng biān)
11. 儿子 (ér zi)

Down

1. 西北部 (xī běi bù)
2. 大海 (dà hǎi)
3. 德国 (dé guó)
5. 上小学 (shàng xiǎo xué)
6. 在家 (zài jiā)
7. 东南边儿 (dōng nán biān r)
9. 大家 (dà jiā)

100

Across

4. 上星期考试了 (shàng xīng qī kǎo shì le)
6. 几月 (jǐ yuè)
7. 填好了 (tián hǎo le)
8. 走吧 (zǒu ba)
9. 完了 (wán le)
10. 好酒 (hǎo jiǔ)

Down

1. 试一试 (shì yi shì)
2. 他上个月走了 (tā shàng ge yuè zǒu le)
3. 日期 (rì qī)
5. 考得好不好 (kǎo de hǎo bu hǎo)

101

Across

5. 她的车跟我的一样 (tā de chē gēn wǒ de yí yàng)
7. 女校 (nǚ xiào)
8. 说话 (shuō huà)
9. 四点整 (sì diǎn zhěng)

Solutions

xīn nián
10. 新 年

Down

yào mǎi hǎo de
1. 要 买 好 的

zěn me yàng
2. 怎 么 样

nǐ de xué xiào zài nǎ r
3. 你 的 学 校 在 哪 儿

qǐng gēn wǒ shuō
4. 请 跟 我 说

yī jiǔ sì jiǔ nián
6. 一 九 四 九 年

102

Across

qián tiān
2. 前 天

chē piào
4. 车 票

qì xiàng zhàn
5. 气 象 站

nǐ jiào shén me míng zi
7. 你 叫 什 么 名 字

xǐ huan
9. 喜 欢

Down

jīn tiān tiān qì zěn me yàng
1. 今 天 天 气 怎 么 样

qì chē zhàn
3. 汽 车 站

wǒ jiào wáng huān
6. 我 叫 王 欢

zì diǎn
8. 字 典

103

Across

bàn gōng shì zài wǔ lóu
4. 办 公 室 在 五 楼

zài shāng diàn li
6. 在 商 店 里

yǒu shén me fǎ zi
7. 有 什 么 法 子

dǎ wǎng qiú yǒu shén me hǎo
9. 打 网 球 有 什 么 好

suǒ yǐ
10. 所 以

Down

zěn me bàn
1. 怎 么 办

xīng qī wǔ shàng yǔ fǎ kè hǎo
2. 星 期 五 上 语 法 课 好

wò shì
3. 卧 室

gōng yuán li you mei yǒu cè suǒ
5. 公 园 里 有 没 有 厕 所

shàng wǎng
8. 上 网

104

Across

nà běn shū shì xiǎo wáng de
4. 那 本 书 是 小 王 的

dì shàng
6. 地 上

chū guó xué xí
7. 出 国 学 习

yī fu
8. 衣 服

Solutions

huā chá
9. 花 茶

zhè me piào liang de gōng yuán
11. 这 么 漂 亮 的 公 园

Down

tā bú shì měi guó rén
1. 他 不 是 美 国 人

kè běn
2. 课 本

nǚ wáng
3. 女 王

nà jiàn shàng yī zěn me mài
5. 那 件 上 衣 怎 么 卖

huā yuán
10. 花 园

105

Across

xué xí
2. 学 习

diàn yǐng yuàn
4. 电 影 院

tā xìn shàng shuō shén me
6. 他 信 上 说 什 么

yīng yǔ kè bù nán
8. 英 语 课 不 难

Down

liàn xí
1. 练 习

xué yuàn
3. 学 院

diàn zǐ xìn
5. 电 子 信

shàng hàn yǔ kè
7. 上 汉 语 课

106

Across

wǔ shí
1. 五 十

yǐ jīng bàn ge xiǎo shí le
6. 已 经 半 个 小 时 了

chí dào
7. 迟 到

duō shao
8. 多 少

kè tīng hěn dà
9. 客 厅 很 大

Down

shí èr diǎn bàn zài cān tīng jiàn
2. 十 二 点 半 在 餐 厅 见

nǐ de xiǎo hái duō dà le
3. 你 的 小 孩 多 大 了

wǒ yǐ dào jiā
4. 我 已 到 家

chī le ma
5. 吃 了 吗

107

Across

shàng hǎi huà
1. 上 海 话

dì jiǔ kè de yǔ fǎ hěn nán
5. 第 九 课 的 语 法 很 难

tiān qì yù bào
7. 天 气 预 报

kě yǐ
10. 可 以

shēng rì kuài lè
12. 生 日 快 乐

Solutions

Down

shàng xué dì yī tiān
2. 上 学 第 一 天

é yǔ
3. 俄 语

tài nán le
4. 太 难 了

fǎ lù
6. 法 律

yù xí shēng cí
8. 预 习 生 词

suǒ yǐ
9. 所 以

kě lè
11. 可 乐

108

Across

qǐng jìn
2. 请 进

zhè píng jiǔ bù hǎo hē
4. 这 瓶 酒 不 好 喝

dàn shì
7. 但 是

chá bēi
8. 茶 杯

duō xiè
10. 多 谢

tài dà le
11. 太 大 了

Down

niú nǎi píng
1. 牛 奶 瓶

qǐng hē chá
3. 请 喝 茶

zhè shì wáng tài tai
5. 这 是 王 太 太

bú yòng xiè
6. 不 用 谢

bēi zi
9. 杯 子

109

Across

cóng měi guó jì lái de
4. 从 美 国 寄 来 的

cān jiā
6. 参 加

ná èr shí wǔ běn shū
7. 拿 二 十 五 本 书

fáng zi
9. 房 子

chū lai
10. 出 来

xiě xìn
11. 写 信

Down

gāng cóng jiā ná dà lái
1. 刚 从 加 拿 大 来

chū guó
2. 出 国

huí lai
3. 回 来

jì le wǔ fēng xìn
5. 寄 了 五 封 信

shū fáng
8. 书 房

110

Solutions

Across

1. bù rú
不如

4. suàn yi suàn
算一算

6. bǎ qián gěi sī jī
把钱给司机

9. hái yǒu yí ge
还有一个

Down

2. bú yào qián
不要钱

3. jì suàn jī
计算机

5. suàn le
算了

7. bǎ shū huán le
把书还了

8. gěi tā yí běn
给他一本

---

2. wài dì
外地

3. yí gòng
一共

5. gōng sī jīng lǐ de bàn gōng shì
公司经理的办公室

6. qì yóu
汽油

8. tā zǒu le
他走了

11. shì qing
事情

111

Across

4. dì tiě bǐ gōng gòng qì chē kuài
地铁比公共汽车快

7. yǐ jīng
已经

9. mài piào de
卖票的

10. bàn wán shì le
办完事了

Down

1. zì xíng chē
自行车

112

Across

1. sān ge wèn tí
三个问题

4. xià ge yuè ràng tā qù
下个月让他去

8. shàng lóu
上楼

9. cān jiā
参加

10. bàn gōng shì
办公室

11. měi lì
美丽

12. yì shu
艺术

Down

2. sān ge yuè
三个月

3. wèn wen tā
问问他

5. xià lóu qù bàn shì
下楼去办事

Solutions

6. 让 他 来
ràng tā lái

7. 去 参 观 美 术 馆
qù cān guān měi shù guǎn

113

Across

1. 听 一 听
tīng yi tīng

5. 周 末 快 乐
zhōu mò kuài lè

7. 懂 了
dǒng le

8. 看 不 见
kàn bu jiàn

10. 面 试
miàn shì

11. 网 球 赛
wǎng qiú sài

Down

2. 听 音 乐
tīng yīn yuè

3. 听 不 懂
tīng bu dǒng

4. 上 周
shàng zhōu

6. 快 去 看 比 赛
kuài qù kàn bǐ sài

9. 见 面
jiàn miàn

114

Across

3. 两 本 汉 英 词 典
liǎng běn hàn yīng cí diǎn

5. 这 件 衬 衫 比 那 件 长
zhè jiàn chèn shān bǐ nà jiàn cháng

7. 物 理 课 本
wù lǐ kè běn

8. 贵 国
guì guó

Down

1. 这 本 书 比 那 本 贵
zhè běn shū bǐ nà běn guì

2. 生 词
shēng cí

4. 一 件 礼 物
yí jiàn lǐ wù

6. 长 裙
cháng qún

115

Across

1. 出 发
chū fā

5. 电 话
diàn huà

7. 一 辆 新 车
yí liàng xīn chē

8. 开 飞 机
kāi fēi jī

9. 旅 行
lǚ xíng

10. 车 来 了
chē lái le

Down

2. 出 租 车 开 错 了 路
chū zū chē kāi cuò le lù

3. 谈 话
tán huà

Solutions

wǔ liàng zì xíng chē
4. 五 辆 自 行 车
diàn shì jī
6. 电 视 机

116

Across
bàn hù zhào
1. 办 护 照
yīn yuè jiào shì
5. 音 乐 教 室
xiě zì
8. 写 字
tīng dǒng le
10. 听 懂 了

Down
bàn gōng shì
2. 办 公 室
zhào piàn
3. 照 片
kuài lè
4. 快 乐
yīn xìn
6. 音 信
jiāo hàn zì
7. 教 汉 字
xiě cuò le
9. 写 错 了

117

Across
mǎ shàng
1. 马 上
qí zhe mǎ
3. 骑 着 马

zuò chē lǚ xíng
6. 坐 车 旅 行
hǔ nián
8. 虎 年
zuò diàn tī shàng lóu
9. 坐 电 梯 上 楼

Down
mǎ mǎ hū hū
2. 马 马 虎 虎
qí zi xíng chē shàng bān
4. 骑 自 行 车 上 班
qì chē
5. 汽 车
zuò yi zuò
7. 坐 一 坐
diàn chē
10. 电 车

118

Across
kě yǐ
1. 可 以
kāi wán xiào
4. 开 玩 笑
tīng yīn yuè huì
6. 听 音 乐 会
rén mín bì
9. 人 民 币

Down
kě xiào de rén
2. 可 笑 的 人
bù tīng huà
3. 不 听 话
kāi huì
5. 开 会

Solutions

yuè qì
7. 乐 器

wài bì
8. 外 币

mín zú
10. 民 族

119

Across

yòu shǒu
2. 右 手

wèi shēng jiān zài zuǒ bian
4. 卫 生 间 在 左 边

hē shuǐ
7. 喝 水

kè rén
8. 客 人

píng cháng
9. 平 常

cān tīng
10. 餐 厅

tí gāo
11. 提 高

Down

fáng jiān
1. 房 间

yòu biān shì kè tīng
3. 右 边 是 客 厅

shēng huó shuǐ píng gāo
5. 生 活 水 平 高

zài nǎ r
6. 在 哪 儿

120

Across

kāi xué de shí hou hěn máng
3. 开 学 的 时 候 很 忙

gōng sī
6. 公 司

zuò cuò le shì
7. 做 错 了 事

gōng zuò
9. 工 作

qǐ chuáng
10. 起 床

Down

shàng xué
1. 上 学

yòu shí jiān zuò zuò yè
2. 有 时 间 做 作 业

kāi mén
4. 开 门

máng gōng shì
5. 忙 公 事

liǎo bu qǐ
8. 了 不 起

121

Across

dà xué shēng dōu kàn bào
3. 大 学 生 都 看 报

bàn gōng lóu lí hǎi guān bù
6. 办 公 楼 离 海 关 不
yuǎn
远

zú qiú chǎng
9. 足 球 场

hěn duō tiān yǐ hòu
10. 很 多 天 以 后

Solutions

Down

1. zhōng xué
中 学

2. rì bào
日 报

4. dà xué lí shāng chǎng hěn yuǎn
大 学 离 商 场 很 远

5. kàn de yuǎn
看 得 远

7. bàn shì
办 事

8. guān mén
关 门

11. hòu bian mian
后 边 / 面

122

Across

1. xiān sheng
先 生

6. nán zhǔ jué yǎn de hǎo jí le
男 主 角 演 得 好 极 了

8. yǒu hǎo dà fāng
友 好 大 方

10. xì yuàn
戏 院

Down

2. shēng qì le
生 气 了

3. fáng zhǔ
房 主

4. shàng yǎn dì fāng xì
上 演 地 方 戏

5. ná hǎo piào
拿 好 票

7. nán péng you
男 朋 友

9. hǎo rén
好 人

123

Across

3. zhù nǐ xīn nián kuài lè
祝 你 新 年 快 乐

6. qiān wàn bié zháo jí
千 万 别 着 急

8. máng de bù dé liǎo
忙 得 不 得 了

10. rú guǒ
如 果

11. tóng yì
同 意

12. dāng fān yi
当 翻 译

Down

1. guò nián
过 年

2. yīn yuè
音 乐

4. zhù nǐ wàn shì rú yì
祝 你 万 事 如 意

5. kuài pǎo
快 跑

7. jí máng
急 忙

9. bù gǎn dāng
不 敢 当

124

Solutions

Across

qǔ diào　zi tè bié yōu měi
2. 曲调／子特别优美
qù kàn jīng jù le
5. 去看京剧了
dài shàng dì tú
7. 带上地图
cóng lái méi gěi guò qián
8. 从来没给过钱

Down

yuè qǔ
1. 乐曲
bié wàng le dài qián
3. 别忘了带钱
měi lì de dì fang
4. 美丽的地方
kàn jiàn méi you
6. 看见没有
cóng qián
9. 从前
guò qù
10. 过去

125

Across

shàng xià lóu yòng diàn tī
3. 上下楼用电梯
yóu jú de páng biān shì shāng
6. 邮局的旁边是商
diàn
　店
huí jiā yí ge yuè
8. 回家一个月
zhōng shì yuán lín
9. 中式园林

Down

dà lóu hòu bian yǒu ge huā yuán
1. 大楼后边有个花园
lóu tī
2. 楼梯
shàng bian de guó jiā shì zhōng guó
4. 上边的国家是中国
diàn qì shāng chǎng
5. 电器商场
yóu piào
7. 邮票

126

Across

guò mǎ lù
1. 过马路
tài zhèng shì le
6. 太正式了
tiān qì hěn rè
8. 天气很热
bù xí guàn
10. 不习惯

Down

guò jié
2. 过节
lù shàng tài rè
3. 路上太热
bìng le
4. 病了
lěng tiān
5. 冷天
shì yàng
7. 式样
qì wēn bù gāo
9. 气温不高

Solutions

127

Across

3. 买 房 子
mái fáng zi

5. 毛 笔
máo bǐ

6. 你 比 我 高 两 公 分
nǐ bǐ wǒ gāo liǎng gōng fēn

9. 是 同 一 天 买 的
shì tóng yì tiān mǎi de

11. 花 店
huā diàn

Down

1. 三 毛 五 分
sān máo wǔ fēn

2. 恭 喜 你
gōng xǐ nǐ

4. 房 租 高
fáng zū gāo

7. 我 不 一 定 去
wǒ bù yí dìng qù

8. 公 园 的 花
gōng yuán de huā

10. 是 不 是
shì bu shì

128

Across

2. 计 划
jì huà

4. 放 假 的 打 算
fàng jià de dǎ suan

7. 不 在
bú zài

8. 桌 布
zhuō bù

9. 途 经 香 港
tú jīng xiāng gǎng

11. 椅 子
yǐ zi

12. 上 次 谈 话
shàng cì tán huà

Down

1. 寒 假
hán jià

3. 计 算
jì suàn

5. 放 在 桌 子 上
fàng zài zhuō zi shàng

6. 打 长 途 电 话
dǎ cháng tú diàn huà

10. 香 水
xiāng shuǐ

129

Across

2. 早 上
zǎo shang

4. 进 门
jìn mén

6. 一 场 足 球 比 赛
yī chǎng zú qiú bǐ sài

9. 国 家 队
guó jiā duì

10. 员 工
yuán gōng

12. 人 们
rén men

Solutions

Down

qiú mén
1. 球门
shàng bàn chǎng
3. 上 半 场
jìn le qiú de duì yuán
5. 进 了 球 的 队 员
yí bàn
7. 一 半
sài pǎo
8. 赛 跑
gōng rén
11. 工 人

130

Across

měi nián dōng tiān xià xuě
4. 每 年 冬 天 下 雪
yīn tiān
7. 阴 天
duō cháng shí jiān
8. 多 长 时 间
xià yì zhōu de kè biǎo
11. 下 一 周 的 课 表

Down

qù nián
1. 去 年
xià tiān
2. 夏 天
dà xuě
3. 大 雪
měi ge xiǎo shí chī yí piàn
5. 每 个 小 时 吃 一 片
xià yǔ tiān
6. 下 雨 天

duō yú
9. 多 余
shàng kè
10. 上 课
biǎo yǎn
11. 表 演

131

Across

xī guā
3. 西 瓜
yǒu yì si
5. 有 意 思
shī rén pá cháng chéng
7. 诗 人 爬 长 城
shì zhōng xīn
9. 市 中 心
gāo shān
11. 高 山
dǐng céng
12. 顶 层

Down

huáng guā
1. 黄 瓜
yuàn yì
2. 愿 意
xī fāng rén
4. 西 方 人
yǒu de chéng shì
6. 有 的 城 市
pá shàng shān dǐng
8. 爬 上 山 顶
zhōng wǔ
10. 中 午

Solutions

132

Across

kuàng quán shuǐ
1. 矿 泉 水

zhōng nián rén de shōu rù dī
4. 中 年 人 的 收 入 低

xīn nián
6. 新 年

yí lù píng ān
7. 一 路 平 安

kē jì
9. 科 技

xiě xìn
10. 写 信

cháng lái
11. 常 来

Down

shuǐ píng dī
2. 水 平 低

měi nián yǒu xīn jì shù
3. 每 年 有 新 技 术

shōu dào yì fēng xìn
5. 收 到 一 封 信

píng píng cháng cháng
8. 平 平 常 常

133

Across

yòng diàn nǎo xiě wén zhāng
3. 用 电 脑 写 文 章

tí gāo
6. 提 高

zuò hǎo liǎng piàn miàn bāo
8. 做 好 两 片 面 包

fú wù yuán
11. 服 务 员

gōng rén
12. 工 人

Down

dà nǎo
1. 大 脑

kè wén
2. 课 文

yòng sī chóu zuò yī fu
4. 用 丝 绸 做 衣 服

xiě míng xìn piàn
5. 写 明 信 片

tí bāo
7. 提 包

liǎng wèi yuán gōng
9. 两 位 员 工

miàn tiáo
10. 面 条

134

Across

wǒ duì lǚ yóu gǎn xìng qù
4. 我 对 旅 游 感 兴 趣

yǒu jǐ ge bāo
8. 有 几 个 包

liǎo jiě
9. 了 解

zài jiàn
10. 再 见

miàn tán
11. 面 谈

Down

bú duì
1. 不 对

Solutions

dǎo yóu
2. 导 游

gāo xìng
3. 高 兴

wǒ men jǐ diǎn jiàn miàn
5. 我 们 几 点 见 面

lǚ xíng bāo
6. 旅 行 包

gǎn mào le
7. 感 冒 了

tán huà
12. 谈 话

135

Across

xià jì
2. 夏 季

gēn péng you liáo tiān
4. 跟 朋 友 聊 天

qì hòu
7. 气 候

xiǎo shì
8. 小 事

chū le jiā mén jiù dǎ dī
9. 出 了 家 门 就 打 的

Down

sì jì
1. 四 季

xià tiān qì wēn jiù gāo
3. 夏 天 气 温 就 高

gēn tóng shì chū chāi
5. 跟 同 事 出 差

yǒu hǎo guó jiā
6. 友 好 国 家

dí què
10. 的 确

136

Across

tā qí zhe ma
2. 他 骑 着 马

tā yòng zuǒ shǒu xiě zì
6. 她 用 左 手 写 字

tā bèi zhuàng shāng le
7. 她 被 撞 伤 了

liǎo jiě
9. 了 解

Down

zuò zhe
1. 坐 着

tā de shǒu jī bèi tōu le
3. 他 的 手 机 被 偷 了

mǎ shàng
4. 马 上

bú yòng xiè
5. 不 用 谢

shāng yuán
8. 伤 员

137

Across

ōu yuán
1. 欧 元

yà zhōu
3. 亚 洲

jiè le yí liàng zì xíng chē
6. 借 了 一 辆 自 行 车

kàn shū
8. 看 书

yí gòng duō shǎo rén
9. 一 共 多 少 人

Solutions

tíng chē chǎng
11. 停 车 场

Down

ōu zhōu lǚ xíng tuán shǎo
2. 欧 洲 旅 行 团 少

hǎo le
4. 好 了

wǔ liàng gōng gòng qì chē
5. 五 辆 公 共 汽 车

jiè shū zhèng
7. 借 书 证

rén men
10. 人 们

138

Across

yīn wei
1. 因 为

qíng kuàng zěn me yàng
4. 情 况 怎 么 样

hěn hǎo
5. 很 好

bàn gōng lóu zài shì zhōng xīn
8. 办 公 楼 在 市 中 心

Down

wèi shén me
2. 为 什 么

shì qing bù hǎo bàn
3. 事 情 不 好 办

dà lóu
6. 大 楼

chén shì   dū shì
7. 城 市 / 都 市

gōng yuán
9. 公 园

zài jiā
10. 在 家

zhōng jiān
11. 中 间

139

Across

yí bàn
1. 一 半

yè shì
3. 夜 市

zhēn liǎo bu qǐ
4. 真 了 不 起

tóng shì
6. 同 事

tán tiān
8. 谈 天

wén xué
9. 文 学

qì hòu biàn huà
11. 气 候 变 化

rè qíng
13. 热 情

Down

bàn yè qǐ chuáng
2. 半 夜 起 床

liǎo jiě tiān qì qíng kuàng
5. 了 解 天 气 情 况

tóng xué
7. 同 学

wén huà
10. 文 化

biàn huàn
12. 变 换

Solutions

140

Across

2. zhī dào
知道

3. kàn cài dān
看菜单

5. lěng rè
冷热

8. nào shì qū de pài chū suǒ
闹市区的派出所

11. yòng qì chē
用汽车

12. hè kǎ
贺卡

Down

1. tōng zhī dān
通知单

4. kàn rè nao
看热闹

6. shuí de xìn yòng kǎ
谁的信用卡

7. cè suǒ
厕所

9. shì chǎng
市场

10. chū zū chē
出租车